Preacher Behave:

A Handbook of Ministerial Ethics

D1530889

Preacher Behave:

A Handbook of Ministerial Ethics

J. CLARK HENSLEY

ISBN 0-9658826-4-0

Preacher Behave:
A Handbook of Ministerial Ethics
by J. Clark Hensley

Revised Edition ©2001 by J. Clark Hensley
Illustrations ©2001 by Joe McKeever

Published by The Ministers' Friend
in conjunction with Parrish House Books.
Printed in the United States.

•

This title can be ordered directly from the publisher:
The Ministers' Friend
P.O. Box 1135
Clinton, Mississippi 39060
Phone 601-924-3019
Fax 601-924-9354

•

Cataloging-in-Publication Data
on record with the Library of Congress

DEDICATION

To the Laos – "All the people of God"

We salute the fellowship of believers
whose warmth and witness points people
of all cultures and races to the ONE
who came to redeem and reconcile us all.

Strength for the Journey

"From the rising of the sun to its setting
the name of the Lord is to be praised."
Psalm 113:3

"Every morning lean your arms awhile
upon the window sill of heaven
and gaze upon your Lord.
Then with that vision in your heart,
Turn strong to meet your day."
Anon

ACKNOWLEDGMENTS

I want to extend a special word of gratitude to Dr. W.W. Walley, M.D., for his contribution to this work; to Pastor Charles E. Poole for his encouragement; to Pastor Joe McKeever, definitely a minister's friend, for his insightful cartoons that evoke both humor and challenge; for Jon Parrish Peede, Parrish House Books, for invaluable professional counsel; to Evelyn M. Burke, Pat Jordan, and Shirley Sanders Reid for devoted assistance; to numerous professors and students, ministers, both clergy and laypersons, who have contributed to my seventy-one years of ministerial experience – some contemporary – more in God's grandstand. So as I write, I am compassed about with a great host of witnesses to whom I am debtor!

Finally, to record my thanksgiving to our Father for my beloved Margaret and our extended Hensley-Sipes family whose love, affirmation and tender care continues by the grace of God to make this a delightful journey.

CONTENTS

FOREWORD

"The Kingdom of Heaven is like..., good seed sown in a field..., a grain of mustard seed sown in a field..., leaven which a woman took..., treasure hid in a field..., a net which was thrown in the sea... Have you understood all this?" Jesus asked. When His disciples said, "Yes," He continued, "Therefore every scribe who has been trained for the Kingdom of Heaven is like a house-holder who brings out of his treasure what is new and what is old." Clark Hensley is like that scribe/householder. There are things here both new and old. And all are good! Those of us versed in some of the Christian ways of Latin America understand the need to contextualize, to speak the Gospel in ways both new and old to our hearers and readers. Clark is a contextualizer and a maestro in that art. If you have a copy of that book (*Preacher Behave!*, first edition) out of which this one has grown, compare them. Things both old and new. All GOOD!

Clark and I have been close friends for years more than a quarter century. He has been my guest, and I, his. Our wives have also accepted and loved each other. We feel like family. Indeed, we are family! I have watched him in the classroom, in the pulpit, at table, in the car, in conferences, in close personal conversation (I have even heard him speaking aloud, very aloud, to himself in the next motel room – some might call it snoring). I have talked with him about how he prepared sermons and conference presentations. He has shared dilemma situations, those times in which there seem to be no one, right, it-all-turns-out-for-good answer to agonizing real life challenges. We have all faced them, no matter how we tried to resolve them. Clark is also a maestro in those situations. And many of them are reflected in these pages that you read. My advice to you is, put this book on the shelf with other books, those to which you turn when you need help with things either trivial but important or more portentous.

This book in finely crafted, closely knit and well organized, like Clark and Margaret's lives. Clark may be the only person I know who thinks in outline form immediately, and expresses himself in wonderful prose. Enjoy! I, along with my students and church friends, have done so for years. Join us, Clark's large, extended family.

Dr. Bob E. Adams
Veteran missionary to Latin America
and seminary professor in ethics

PREFACE

"That thou mayest know how thou oughtest to behave thyself in the house of God, which is the church of the living God, the pillar and ground of the truth."
1 Timothy 3:15

"If you continue to teach these things, you shall be a good minister of Jesus Christ, ever feeding your own soul on the truths of the faith and of the fine teaching which you have followed."
1 Timothy 4:6 (Author's translation, hereafter JCH)

In this discussion we shall consider "minister," "preacher" and "pastor" synonymously. Though we may often use the pronouns "he," we do not presume that a minister must be male. We will not quibble over whether others are called to the work nor split hairs over who is a minister, but rather express views that I hope are in keeping with the mind of Christ on the pressing question: *How should a preacher behave?*

Should his practices be any different from other Christian people? What are some of his *peculiar* temptations to veer from the highest ethical standards in his conduct toward his family, his flock, his friends, his community, his fellow pastors and others? Accepting the biblical teaching concerning the priesthood of the believer, the authority of the scriptures, the leadership of the Holy Spirit and the Lordship of Christ, I would not expect each minister to agree with all that is said here but would hope each to respectfully consider what is presented. Dealing with ethical decisions involves judgment as to what the Bible teaches as well as how we are to live it out in our practice.

Believe and behave is my admonition. Speaking in love what I perceive to be the truth is my aim. To help build each other up is my objective.

Dr. Bob E. Adams defines ethics as "responsible action on the part of man in a community setting. Christian ethics is responsible action on the part of a Christian man in a community setting." It follows then that ministerial ethics refers to responsible action on the part of a Christian minister in the family, church, and community setting.

When thinking about our relationship to others as ministers, "to edify the body of Christ" is the goal. Christ-mindedness should be our attitude and Christian behavior the method. The essential objective of the work must be that of effective spiritual leadership. This involves not only what he teaches but how he *practices* what he teaches.

Rationale for Congregational Ethics and the Minister's Friend

The ethics of our American culture seems to have degenerated on all fronts. Ageism, Racism, Consumerism, Instant Gratification are all a part of the seductive web. Politics has become a game for position and power. Character assassination is the popular method for advantage and destroying one's opponents. The term *dirty politics* can be translated *deadly politics.* Lying, cheating or stealing – any way to win and use position with eye upon the next election with more false promises.

While giving a political speech on a country radio station, one candidate was harshly lambasting his opponent's views, almost to the point of slander when he stopped abruptly. Speaking in milder tones he continued, "Now, folks, please don't misunderstand me. Judge Jones and I are deacons in the same church. We have been close friends but political enemies for years!"

Entertainment has been taken over by those whose ethics are at the lowest common denominator of excess in sensualism. Sports are the most obscene with the power of money, violence and hero worship of those who cheat, taunt and injure.

Instant gratification of any desire – "If it feels good, do it." "What is yours is mine if I want it." No respect for property rights or privacy. By deceitful false advertising the health of the nation is jeopardized.

Cheap imitations and faulty merchandise weaken trust and sometimes imperil safety. Situation ethics or what is expedient colors the pattern.

Many of these *values* carry over into churches and religious groups. Some ministers may be tempted to resort to hypocrisy, manipulation, coercion and favoritism. Charles Colson has said, "American culture ethics must be repudiated and changed if America is to survive."

Too many ministers are losing their positions as a result of some conflict with the members or in some struggle between members. Though always played up by the media, not often does a minister relinquish his/her position for some immoral act or character flaw. Charges are made. The gossip mongers in mock concern spell out details in public requests for prayer, and the minister seems helpless. The minister's family is disrupted. Children are disappointed in their *friends*. School work suffers. Parents grieve and prayerfully try to *find God's will.* Often, the minister turns to some other career because his reputation has been tainted by his resignation without *somewhere to go.* It is an ugly picture, and the blame game does not help. God is not honored as churches suffer disrespect by non-church goers.

Preacher Behave, according to testimonies of hundreds, has alerted many young and inexperienced ministers to the ethical relationships that must be faced personally and within the membership and community. This revised edition is directed to all ministers and all members of all denominations. It includes a section on *Congregational Ethics and how the members ought to behave to be the minister's friend.*

Better communication between ministers and their congregation should develop better understanding to diffuse and settle differences with civility. The practice of the best ethical relationships will increase the respect of the community for the minister and the congregation. As the title suggests, the basic reason for this revision is to give practical pointers to the inexperienced minister. Many honest ministers on being asked the key to a fruitful life could reply, "Well, for one thing, at a critical time I had a Friend."

I have observed the respect, love and friendship most congregations have toward their minister. So I write as a minister's friend with concern for the congregations of the Lord's people that together we may honor Him who said, "You are my friends, if you do what I command you. Love one another."

"GOOD EVENING, BISHOPS, SUPERINTENDENTS, EXECUTIVE DIRECTORS, DIRECTORS OF MISSIONS, DENOMINATIONAL LEADERS, SENIOR PASTORS, MISSIONARIES, ASSOCIATE PASTORS, EXECUTIVE PASTORS, EDUCATIONAL MINISTERS, MUSIC MINISTERS, STUDENT PASTORS, CHILDREN'S MINISTERS, BUSINESS MANAGERS, MINISTERS OF PASTORAL CARE, AND DIRECTORS OF EVANGELISM. WELL, I SEE MY TIME IS UP!"

1.
THE MINISTER'S FAMILY

God expects us to have enough of heaven in our homes here to get us a little bit prepared for what Heaven is going to be like when we arrive there.

If a pastor has a Messiah complex, his home life will suffer. When one becomes a workaholic, he will neglect his wife and children. It is a sad day when a pastor's child calls the office to say, "Daddy, when can I get an appointment with you?" or just as tragic when the youngster feels that "Dad never has time for me – always time for everyone else, but never for me." Dad is off on an ego-massage trip instead of attending the Little League game.

Sometimes it's the pastor's wife who is driving her husband to court the favor of others, to gain prestige in order to get a *bigger church*. She may salve her conscience by telling him, "You have much more to offer than those people will take," ad nauseam.

Setting the Pace

How should, or can, a minister set the pace for the family? He can, if he will, take a day off. He can work with his family toward a family night at home. He can take a time alone mini-vacation with his wife at least once in three months. He should freely explain to his congregation how he is trying to model a good home life before his people.

It is necessary for ministers and their families to have some close friends. Some find it possible to do this among their own members. Others frown upon too much socializing with only a few in the church. Perhaps they could well be chosen from other denominations, the families of other ministers of their own faith, or among community groups within which one makes acquaintances. It is often a possible and happy situation to maintain some friendships with folk from former pastorates. In such event, one would never be critical of the present pastor or his family.

The minister's home, like others, needs the security of a dependable routine. One should exercise care to keep mealtime hours and other appointments with the family. They should be given equal consideration with other church family members. One can ethically plead a previous engagement to keep such appointments. Maintaining a proper balance between the demands of other families and the needs of his own family should be his goal.

The telephone may be one of the worst offenders in infringement upon family time. The minister should develop the art of terminating conversations. It is not bad manners to terminate a telephone conversation. For example, one might say:

"It was nice of you to call. Call again sometime."

"Thank you for letting me know. I'll see what I can do. Goodbye."

"I'm busy just now. When can we get together to talk about this?"

"Suppose I call you back at four o'clock. Will that be convenient?"

"We are eating just now. May I return your call in twenty minutes or so?"

"We are leaving for an appointment. I'll call you tomorrow."

"I'm helping Lisa with her homework. Let me call you back at eight. OK?"

"It is always good to hear from you. You are so thoughtful. We often thank God for you. Call again when you can. Goodbye."

"I'd like to give this my best attention and I believe it is going to take longer than I have just now. Can you call me at the office at nine in the morning?"

The Minister and Vacations

It is unethical for a minister not to take a vacation. He is being unfair to his membership, himself and his family. He is being a poor steward of resources that God has given him. If Jesus found it necessary to go apart and rest a while, what minister could be so arrogant as to believe that he does not need a period of rest and recuperation?

How long should a vacation period be? This should be ascertained by the church before the minister accepts the pastorate. In some sections of the country, vacations are from two to three months in length – a portion of the time, of course, to be given to study, sermon preparation and planning for the new year. It is more like a mini-sabbatical. Others would find difficulty in being away from the pulpit that long. Some feel that the vacation period should be split – that is, a period in the summer and a period in the winter. However, families with children in school may have problems with this.

We have already advocated that the minister should take mini-vacations with his wife – a couple of days or so every three months. But this is not to be confused with a more lengthy vacation period which is essential for one to really get away and rest from the routine.

Some churches and church organizations have a two-week vacation period for the first five years, lengthen this to three weeks for the next five years, and after ten years of service, a month. The pastor needs to remember that most of his parishioners will not receive more than two weeks and may find it hard to understand why the pastor needs more than a month.

Whatever time is allowed for vacation should be used for vacation. Too many ministers use their vacation time for additional revival meetings or other strenuous efforts. The necessity of added remuneration may be involved, and this is certainly understandable. However, the minister who uses vacation time for anything other than vacation ought to consider the ethics of such behavior. Could it mean that he doesn't need it? If he doesn't need it, should he accept it?

Modern Baal Worship?

Baal worship involved sexual license for the purpose of ritual in the worship of idols. Most ministers would never think of being unfaithful to their spouse with another person. Instead, their unfaithfulness is reflected in their marriage to the church (though the church is said to be the bride of Christ). When the wife is prostituted by being made a thing in order to achieve goals, enhance the image or lift the status of the pastor, he makes an idol of his position *in the name of the Lord*. Sexual license is carried on in the name of marriage when he acts as though his wife and other family members exist for the institutional church. Thus the family is prostituted with the pious phrase *putting the Lord first*, which equates the church programs, activities and schedules with the Lord. Could it be that this combination of idol worship and prostitution is modern Baal worship and just as *unfaithful* as adultery in the sexual sense?

Communication at Home

The minister would do well to give much attention to communication at home. Some who are constant communicators on the outside find it difficult to relate to persons in a closer and more intimate relationship. One of the most frequent complaints of pastors' wives is *"He won't listen to me."* Some pastors constantly operate in an authorization role that carries over to the wife at home. If one, however, is seeking to have a partnership marriage, as I believe the Bible teaches, the husband should not want to boss or be bossed, but to have a mate – a true companion who does not lose her personhood. Unfortunately, there have been many diabolical modes of conduct suggested by ministers under the guise of *"You should obey me."*

There are suggestions in the New Testament for family relationships indicating the direction in which God is carrying His people. God works with people where they are and moves them along to where He wants them to be. There is no God-given or prescribed role structure revealed in the Bible, but the Bible is clear on God's intention for an ideal family relationship.

Paul declared the equality of men and women in redemption (Gal. 3:28-29) and also understood the freedom we have in Christ (II Cor. 3:17-18). He noted that Jesus did not change God's original intention for the family.

3

He began with His hearers' understanding of the traditional marriage.

Here follows a scriptural exposition of the Ephesian pattern of husband-wife relationships upon which ethical patterns are built. Obviously, any variation from this New Testament pattern will involve a difference in how husbands and wives behave toward each other.

The Ephesian Passage

The new ideal presented by Paul was that Christian marriage was similar to the relationship between Christ and the church, characterized by:

1. Mutual submission out of reverence for Christ: "subjecting yourselves to one another in the fear of Christ" (Eph. 5:21). This concept applies to all family members.

Concerning the term usually translated *submit*, John H. Yoder, a Mennonite theologian, states, "It is not best rendered by subjection, which carries a connotation of being thrown down and run over, not by submission, with its connotation of passivity. Subordination means the acceptance of an order, as it exists, but with new meaning given to it by the fact that one's acceptance of it is willing and meaningfully motivated" (Yoder, *The Politics of Jesus.* Erdmans, 1972. pg. 175).

The early Christians had a new kind of dignity and responsibility to each other. In this light and in terms of the root meaning of the word used, translated *submit*, Ephesians 5:21 could read:

"Honor Christ by yielding in love to each other."

"Honor Christ by cooperating intelligently with each other."

"Honor Christ by having an orderly arrangement with each other."

"Honor Christ by reaching consensus with each other."

2. Husband-Wife relationships.

Wives should be responsive to the husband's leadership. "Wives...to your own husbands as to the Lord" (Eph. 5:22).

Responsiveness to leadership requires mutual submission. "For the husband is head of the wife as Christ is head of the church, himself the savior of the body" (Eph. 5:23).

a. Christ exercised His headship by giving up any glories of leadership and not grasping them (see Philippians 2:6-8).

b. His submission to the Father was between equals. It was not that of inferior to superior. Neither is the husband superior to the wife nor the wife superior to the husband.

c. Submission must be voluntary. Though Christ has the power, it is inconceivable that he would coerce or manipulate the church. Likewise, it seems inconceivable that the Christian husband would coerce the wife or the Christian wife would try to manipulate the husband.

3. When the relationship is as above described, the wife does not fear being open to and trusting her husband in everything. "But as the church is subject to Christ, so the wives also to their husbands in everything" (Eph. 5:24).

4. Husbands – love, not control.

a. Self-sacrificing. "Husbands, love your wives even as Christ also loved the church and gave himself up for it" (Eph. 5:25).

b. Cleansing kind of love. The husband is to be an example of holiness. There's a sense in which self-giving, affirming love challenges other family members to purify or keep spiritually clean their relationships (Eph. 5:26-27).

c. Cherishing love – caring as for his own body – a nourishing, building-up kind of love. "Even so ought husbands also to love their own wives as their own bodies. He that loveth his own wife loveth himself: for no man ever hateth his own flesh, but nourisheth and cherisheth it" (Eph. 5:28-29).

d. Committed love. "For this cause will a man leave his father and mother and shall cleave to his wife and the two shall become one flesh" (Eph. 5:32). Each marriage is a unique union demanding commitment.

5. Mutual submission means mutual respect and trust. "Let the wife see that she fear (respect) her husband" (Eph. 5:33). Through the Ephesian passage, one feels the nature of the reciprocal relationship between husband and wife. One does not love and the other submit. Both love, trust and respect.

6. Sexual union in marriage requires mutual submission. "Let the husband render unto the wife her due: and likewise also the wife unto her husband. The wife hath not power over her own body, but the husband: and likewise also the husband hath no power over his own body, but the wife" (I Cor. 7:3-4).

7. Manipulation is ruled out. I Peter 3:1-2 is addressed to women whose husbands are disobedient to the Lord and suggests they are to avoid playing God but allow the Holy Spirit to bring conviction by their reverent and chaste behavior. This passage by no means suggests that the wife should obey her husband and participate in activities that would compromise or nullify her Christian witness.

The Emerging Pattern

Today, in our culture, there is emerging a pattern from the New Testament ideal that may be described by such phrases as interpersonal relationship, mutual affection, mutual trust, mutual respect, companionship, friendship. As David and Vera Maces say: "Marriage in the past was held

5

together by external coercion. Today it can be held together only by internal cohesion" (see Mace, *We Can Have Better Marriages If We Want Them*. Abingdon Press, 1974).

To summarize these New Testament principles for models of marriage relationships:

1. The relationship must be arrived at by consensus. We usually begin by mutually deciding to marry.

2. It must not destroy the personhood of either. As one man said, "I love my wife too much to make her a second class citizen, and that would not make me look good either."

3. One does not manipulate or blackmail by use of power, sex, money or some supposed authority.

4. The marriage partners, if Christians, must consider the Lordship of Christ. He is the Head, the Leader!

5. The skill in Christian marriage lies in communication and negotiation in mutual love.

In the partnership marriage, each partner is free to grow. There is a merging without a submerging. Both partners *grow in oneness*, to use Dr. John Howell's phrase. (Howell, *Growing in Oneness*. Convention Press, 1972). Since marriages are not static, each partner continues working to build a dynamic, growing relationship. While companionship and sharing feed on togetherness, there should be spaces in our togetherness as we all have the need for some privacy. Husband and wife talk time (not just debriefing from the day's events but a genuine sharing of things that matter much) will contribute to building communication patterns and help develop a sensitivity to and response to feelings. Other means of negotiation and communication are family council, family night at home, once-a-week date that may have to be Saturday morning breakfast at a restaurant, and the mini-vacation concept.

Parental Modeling

A plaque in my office reads: "The most important thing a father can do for his children is to love their mother."

Parents should be aware of the example they set in the home, especially in modeling tenderness, compassion, courtesy, kindness, tolerance of each other's views, affectionate gestures, and the handling of conflict or problems. Seeing how parents relate to each other and their children will do more teaching than a lifetime of sermons.

A comment often heard from pastors' wives in the counselor's room is "My husband is not affectionate; he shows but little warmth and tenderness to me or the children." They often add, "He comes from a home where little affection is openly demonstrated in the family." So this pattern of coldness is perpetuated by a failure in modeling. The man of the cloth who claims to know the warmth and comfort of God's love can, if he will, *learn* how to demonstrate love in his own home setting and thus break the perpetuation of what may be less desirable behavior patterns in terms of mental health for the pastor's family.

"Preachers' Kids Can Be Normal"

In *Church Administration* magazine John Warren Steen wrote a very helpful article under this title. He pointed to some of the dangers that preachers face with their children:

• *Divine Obligation.* Brother Average feels uptight about the divine obligation to be "one that ruleth well his own house" (I Tim. 3:4). He seldom stops to think that the word *rule* implies management and organization – not a dictatorship that produces perfection. The Scriptures teach a home relationship built on mutual love and respect. But the New Testament recognizes human imperfection while holding up the ideal of godly perfection.

• *No Spotlight on the Kids.* The pastor who constantly tells cute stories about his children gradually cuts out a pattern that the kids must fit. Either they will strive to top their last clever saying with a better one, or they will resent the false expectations of the listeners to hear them say something witty or profound. Most children harbor a deep resentment about being pushed into the spotlight by a backstage mama or papa. Sometimes the parent commits such a child-battering action because he or she has a secret, unfulfilled desire to receive applause as a musician or a comedian.

Sometimes the congregation will shine a well-meaning spotlight on the youngster despite a parent's best intentions.

• *Confusion of Values.* When a young person's activities are judged on the criterion of what the deacons would say, the child gets mixed up. He doesn't learn intrinsic lessons of whether an action is right or wrong, but he learns a deceptive kind of expediency. The preacher's child finds the going rough when some *Pharisees* in the membership will allow their own teenagers to engage in certain activities but expect the preacher's child to be different, or as they express it, "to set an example for our children." So the preacher's kid, although he doesn't have many other virtues, will usually develop one quality that Jesus had – he can spot a hypocrite a mile away.

Say *church* to many a minister's child and he'll think of a monster. A pastor's son may not think of that loving fellowship of Christians; he may call to mind that organization that expects Daddy to miss *my ball game* on a summer evening to attend a nominating committee meeting or to miss the PTA program in order to go to a cottage prayer meeting. You can almost hear the child saying, "The church is a vampire that sucks the blood out of my daddy."

• *Target for Criticism.* Some church members assume they have a hunting license for criticism. They know anytime is an open season for the pastor's family, and the preacher's boys and girls are sitting ducks. They train their sights on them and seldom miss these vulnerable targets.

Dr. Steen suggests these guidelines to consider to protect ministers and their children from these problems:

• Know who are you are.
• Level with your child.
• Maintain privacy.
• Put your child's welfare above public opinion.
• Build a church atmosphere of acceptance.
• Respect individuality.
• Give freedom.

Dr. Steen concludes with the following comments:

There Are Advantages. In many ways, parsonage kids are pretty lucky. Look at *Who's Who,* and you will discover more sons and daughters of clergymen than any other profession. Most people have a profound love and respect for their pastor and his family. There are people in the congregation who yearn to be grandparents to the P.K.s whose real grandparents are many miles away. They will take the children fishing or golfing. They'll report to you if the youngster on a bike seems to have lost her way or ridden too far from the pastorium. Most children of the parsonage are blessed with everything from football passes to scholarship aid. So the situation is not too bleak after all.

Crisis Periods

The minister's marriage is not immune to crisis periods. Usually they include:

Cleavage crisis – emotionally leaving the parental home.

Coital crisis – sexual adjustment.

Coin crisis – making the budget work.

Clock and calendar crisis – adjusting from the routine of "leisure together" to "work together."

Critical analysis – when one learns to accept weaknesses as well as strengths.

Cooperative role adjustment – from "Mother did this" and "Dad did that" to "What will *our* roles be?"

Church expectations versus our plans.

Church first – "organizational man syndrome."

Coming of the first child – planned or unplanned.

Children-suffering – pains and problems of parenting.

Conflict – learning to cope constructively.

Creative closeness in the empty nest.

Commitment – at a time of some identity crisis or during a period of emotional exhaustion one is more vulnerable.

Communication is the key to handling each *passage* or *stage* – to mention titles that define the process. Books on communication should be read and discussed. Marriage and family enrichment seminars could well be a part of annual activities. Many bookstores and denominational publishers carry helpful materials on these crisis situations.

The Minister's Home

The minister has an ethical obligation to the family to see that the home furnished by the church fits them or that other provisions are made. This cannot always be done satisfactorily at first, but an understanding can be had that adjustments will be made as soon as feasible.

The minister's family should care for any furniture, appliances, drapes, rugs and other items that are furnished by the church as if they were their own. The same would be true for the yard and a garden, if such is provided. Understanding should be had prior to the pastor's going to a church field as to who's responsible for repairs, maintenance, utility bills and related matters.

Is there a guest room furnished in the minister's home that is supposed to be used for the entertainment of visiting church guests, or is the pastor's home considered his own with the right to determine whether or not he wants to invite church guests to be in his home? There should be the opportunity for privacy, with hooks on the screens and locks on the doors. In some rural or small town areas, it is still customary to keep doors unlocked, and there can be many invasions of privacy if the church is located next to the pastor's home. In this situation, a pastor and his wife can sometimes train members to respect their privacy yet feel welcome at certain appropriate times.

The question of the study location in the pastor's home may need to be considered. It could be that the new pastor does not have enough bedroom space and needs to locate his study elsewhere. Is it advisable to have his study away from the office where he can have privacy and be better protected for study periods? Advance understanding in all of these matters will provide better opportunity for the minister's family to behave appropriately in the light of the expectations of the congregation and what they feel best for their own needs.

An appropriate prayer for the minister could well be, "O Lord, how I need your help, especially in my own home where I long to behave as I should" (Ps. 101:2 adapted). But for our comfort and strength we do know: "My God in his tender mercy will meet me at every corner" (Ps. 59:10 adapted).

2.

THE MINISTER'S HEALTH

by W. W. Walley, M.D.

I speak from the vantage point of more than fifty years in the private practice of medicine which most would call a solo practice but which I like to refer to as a partnership, with the Lord Jesus Christ as the senior partner. Because of my commitment to Him and the work of His church, I have treated more than my share of ministers of all faiths and have reached some private conclusions from these experiences. I believe that a man who is truly God-called for a specific task is virtually indestructible until the task is completed or the person strays from his calling. This, however, does not preclude sickness or suffering which come from abusing our bodies.

Foodaholics

We who are believers and abstainers are quick to condemn someone who has allowed alcohol to take control of his body. We call him an alcoholic. But what about people who eat until they become extremely overweight? We refer to them as being obese; I call them *foodaholics*. This is a common *preacher* disease. An extremely overweight person cannot be very efficient. Furthermore, contrary to public opinion, fat people are not always jolly but are often depressed. They've just learned to put on a good front.

It is difficult for an overweight minister to lose weight because everywhere he goes people look at him and assume, correctly so, that he is a big eater. Then they offer larger portions of foods which are often high in calories. If you are not overweight, do not let yourself become so. If you are overweight, get your doctor to prescribe a low calorie diet for you and resolve to stay with it. I believe that there is a personal Satan just as sure as there is a personal Holy Spirit. Perhaps your prayer should be, "Help me, Lord. The Devil wants me fat."

The sin of gluttony is one that, I dare say, very few of you have chosen as a sermon subject. Maybe you should consider this, for truly our bodies are the temple of the Holy Spirit, and we have an awesome responsibility in this regard. When we overeat, we not only harm our bodies and decrease our effectiveness as witnesses, but we also may be depriving someone else of needed food.

11

Workaholics

I want to comment on one other type of addiction, which is seen most commonly in your preachers but is not limited to them. I refer to the person who, perhaps for the first time, comes to the full realization of the overwhelming number of unsaved persons and personally resolves, either consciously or unconsciously, to save the world and thus becomes a *workaholic*. Such a person is often unable to cope with the awareness that he had made an impossible commitment, and can become emotionally upset to the point of being a nervous wreck. This drive and this desire is commendable, but the task is impossible. Not even the teachings of Christ indicate that *all will be saved*. Surely Jesus does not want you to break yourself in the attempt. Jesus wants you to be *well*, and you can do more in the long run for Him if you learn to pace yourself.

Worry

I often see ministers who complain of not being able to sleep or not being able to eat. Very frequently I hear, "Everything I eat gives me indigestion." This means only one thing: You are taking your troubles to bed with you. I know this because I have been there. The best advice I was ever given was by a saintly old doctor who was in the twilight of a long, useful, and highly successful life devoted to God and the practice of medicine. His advice was "Don't take you patients to bed with you. I mean this both ways." I would like to admonish you as servants of God likewise, "Don't take your work to bed with you. When you come to the end of a day's work, accept Christ's invitation to lay all your care and burdens on Him, and if you have done your best, He will take care of you. When you learn to do this, you will sleep well, wake refreshed, and be more alert at the task to which you have been called. You will work with renewed vigor and, in the long run, accomplish much more."

Worry is closely related to what I have referred to above, but it is so important that I think it deserves special emphasis. Worry is a sin in that it makes God a liar. We are told that if we simply turn to Him, He will take care of us. Worry is futile in that at least 40% of the cases the object of our worry never comes to pass. In fully another 30% we cannot change the condition, no matter what we do. In 10% the worry is needless and includes such things as how I look and "What will they say or think?" Another 12% of our worries concerns the state of our health, which is needless. This leaves 8% of our worries that may have some reality about them. In the final analysis, the only thing about which we should really worry is our salvation. If one is not born again and does not have his name inscribed in the Lamb's Book of Life, then he should really be worried.

Fasting

Another thought on the way a preacher should behave concerns fasting and praying. This seems to be an almost completely neglected source of power that was used by all the prophets and by Jesus Christ Himself. I do not know why this is neglected in our day. I have never heard a minister even suggest this, much less heard a sermon preached on it.

I have fasted on several occasions, usually for short periods of time and always for a specific purpose. My longest fast was for ten days, and I want to share with you some of the experiences that I had on this occasion. The most unexpected phenomenon was that at the end of 48 hours, all sensation of hunger disappeared. I am not sure, but I suspect this is due to the depletion of carbohydrates and the switching over to use stored fat as a source of energy. This period was followed by about 48 hours of weakness, then a return of strength. About this same time I was aware of the presence of the Holy Spirit such as I had not known since the day of my conversion. This persisted until the end of the fast. I do not how long the lack of hunger would have lasted, but I suspect it would have continued as long as my body was burning fat. If this assumption is correct, when all stored fat is consumed and the body starts to utilize protein, then hunger will return. If so, the return of hunger is the signal to end the fast.

I emphasize fasting here for two reasons: (1) It can aid in recapturing an awareness of the Holy Spirit and provide a setting for prayer from which spiritual accomplishments can be realized beyond your fondest dreams; and (2) it is the most effective way I know to regain control of your appetite and have a chance to reprogram that computer we call our brain. I challenge you to try it. There is nothing magic about ten days. You won't need that long, but you should go at least four days to overcome both the hunger and the weakness and to experience that awareness of the Holy Spirit that is close kin to euphoria. If you have health problems, you will, of course, want to consult your physician before beginning a fast.

Relax

It has long been my honest opinion that the old adage *all work and no play* really *does* make *Johnny a dull boy*. This holds true for the minister also. You simply MUST have some leisure time – a time to get away from it all and just relax by doing something you really enjoy doing. I don't mean by this that you should drive over to the next town, look up Brother Joe and say, "Well, Joe, how did things go in your church last Sunday?" or "How are things in your church field?" I mean get away and put the church completely our of your mind for a few days or a few hours.

I have heard it said that Christians don't have fun. If you believe this, you have never been on a holiday with Christians. My wife and I, a couple from southwest Mississippi, and a couple from North Carolina make it a point to get together two or three times a year, usually for two or three days at a time, and we truly have Christian fellowship and as much fun as people can have during this time. As much as is humanly possible, I forget about sick people; one of the other couples forgets that there's furniture to be sold; and the other couple lets the manufacturing of fertilizer take care of itself. None of us could do this if we went away with people in our own profession.

In addition to this, you need a hobby – something you can turn to for a few minutes or a few hours periodically to get your mind on something else. The field here is wide open – coin collecting, stamp collecting, study in some field unrelated to church work, etc. The important thing is that you enjoy doing it and it is something you can *lose yourself in* for a little while. You simply must have some leisure time if you are to survive.

Exercise

Exercise is essential to good health and good health is essential to a sound body; never forget that your body is the temple of the Holy Spirit, and always treat it as such. For exercise to be effective, it has to be consistent. A good exercise program is not something you do once or twice a week, but must be done daily if you are to get the maximum benefit. Walking at a good fast pace is a good exercise for your muscles. If you want to exercise for improving your heart, you have to do something that will speed your heart rate up to at least 150 beats per minute. Before you do this, I advise clearance with your personal physician. Walk from home to the office. Walk when you make your pastoral calls and if at all feasible, walk when you go to the hospital to make your visits. (An unanticipated plus to your exercise program is that this is a time when you can get in some *good thinking*.) Anything you do to improve your physical stamina will also improve your ministry – and this is what it's all about.

In summary then, the way a minister should behave from a health standpoint is that he should claim all the promises of Christ. Cast all your worries on Him and do all things in moderation, being always mindful that Jesus wants you well. Also, remember that Satan is real and will always be trying to enter your consciousness in many ways, not the least of which are doubts about your physical well-being.

3.
THE MINISTER'S INTEGRITY

"A Christian has no right anywhere or under any circumstances to be anything less than a Christian."
Frances Wayland

Provide for Things Honest in the Sight of All

Confidential is confidential. Counseling secrets are kept just that. The pastor's wife should not know. The counselee's spouse should not know. None other should know. Other professionals should know only with permission. You may feel obligated to report briefly to those who make referrals to you; just still, confidential is confidential.

One thing about which the pastor should be exceedingly careful is using illustrations from counseling situations. Some pastors try to camouflage such illustrations, but it is unethical to use them unless permission is granted. Even then they should be put in a different setting. It is sad that some pastors can't be trusted. The people sense this and consequently hesitate to go to them about confidential matters.

The Pastor, Confidentiality Law and Help for Counselees

As inferred, it is generally assumed that what is told a minister in the privacy of a counseling session is deemed confidential. In recent years, however, courts of law have not always honored this unless the state has a confidentiality law that specifically covers ministers. The minister should assure the member that as far as he personally is concerned, what is being told him will be held in the strictest confidence. If the state does not have a confidentiality law and there is any possibility of his being subpoenaed into court to give testimony, in all fairness he should caution the member that while many judges will excuse the minister from giving testimony on matters given to him in confidence, this is not always the case, and that this will be the only possible exception to his breaking confidentiality. What a minister is told does not usually involve anything of this nature.

Suppose he is told something that leads him to believe that someone's life is in danger or that the person is suicidal. Does he have the ethical responsibility of warning the person whose life may be in danger, especially if proximity to the person making the threat would enable him to carry it out most any time? Does the minister have ethical responsibility to warn members of the counselee's family that he should be carefully observed and perhaps not left alone for a period of time? Should he suggest to family members that they encourage psychiatric care of the counselee? Should he suggest that the member is severely emotionally disturbed and needs the protection of loving concern and care at this time? Is it advisable to seek the counselee's permission to take other members of the family into their confidence? Suppose a family member is aware of a counseling session and calls the pastor to learn what was said. While he should not reveal details, he could make suggestions as to how help could be given.

There is usually a way to get help for a member without divulging confidences. But the pastor cannot assume responsibility for the conduct of the person or the results of that conduct. Neither can he force one to accept his line of thinking – which leads us to another subject.

Other Pointers on Counseling

In this treatise it is not our purpose to discuss counseling techniques except in terms of ethical procedures. In counseling, however, the minister is desiring to get at five fundamental questions:

1. What is the problem? As the British say – sort it out. Whose problem is it?

2. What are the responsible alternatives?

3. What resources of time, energy, money and opportunity does the member have to proceed on any one of the alternatives?

4. What is right in the situation?

5. What first step can the counselee make to be able to carry out the desired course of conduct?

It is unethical, even as an authority figure, to say, "If I were you, I would do thus and so." You really don't know what you would do if you were this person. It is highly unethical to discourage the use of prescription drugs. It is ethical to encourage a person to get a medical and dental checkup if they haven't had one recently.

It is unethical, and maybe even illegal, to give legal advice, though it could be appropriate for the minister to say, "This is the way I understand the law; however, I suggest that you check with your attorney about this and certainly, I am not giving you legal advice."

What about the ethics of questioning the integrity of some other minister or other church member? Or what about the ethics of planting doubts in the member's mind concerning denominational people such as seminary professors or the orthodoxy of denominational literature? What of the ethics of questioning a man's theological stance because he happens to be liberal or non-cooperative in his views as to the place of minority ethnic groups in the community?

The minister needs to know his limits as a counselor, and some have called this awareness the "art of referral." The minister's goal when referring someone should be to:

1. Instill hope;
2. Give the member adequate information about the agency or person to whom you are referring;
3. Assure your continuing support;
4. Foster realistic expectations; and
5. Help the member understand that getting help is a normal decision.

Who should a minister refer?

1. Those who need medical care and/or institutionalization.
2. Those who need *intensive* individual, marital or family therapy which perhaps surpasses your time or training or both.
3. Those with problems for which effective specialized community agencies are available.
4. Those who abuse alcohol or other substances (unless you are a recovering addict and thus can speak to this condition based upon your own experience).
5. Those who are severely depressed and/or suicidal.
6. Those about the nature of whose problem you are in doubt. Second opinion?
7. Those who do not respond to your help after a few sessions or have a neurotic need for attention.

Honesty in Business Dealings

It is very unfortunate that ministers have a bad reputation about paying their debts. Let us hope that this is sort of a cultural myth and that ministers are doing better these days. Yet I have banker friends tell me about the difficulty they have collecting debts or even getting ministers to acknowledge their obligations. Surely it is a sin to contract for something you cannot pay for. Sometimes there are providential circumstances that change a financial situation so that one cannot pay as promised, but he can still meet his obligations. That is, he can acknowledge the statement and talk with the banker or creditor about his change of circumstances and work out with him something that is mutually satisfactory. One should be careful about getting overextended. Sometimes it is necessary for the wife to work outside the home or for the minister to do moonlighting to be able to make a go of it. If you know you cannot meet your needs from pastoral support, inform your congregation and tell them that, as an honorable person, you expect to meet these needs some other way and will not expect criticism when you do moonlighting, or sunlighting, to make things go right. "If any provide not for his own, especially for those of his own house, he hath denied the faith, and is worse than an infidel" (I Tim. 5:8).

Favors, Gifts and Discounts

What about the acceptance of favors, gifts and discounts? Surely a pastor would not ask or even hint for such. There are some people who want to give out of their love, and to deprive them of this privilege would not be right; but some will give as power plays. The pastor should be very careful not to be *bought off.* He may find himself silenced on some issue later because he has accepted favors from a member who is trying to buy his influence. Sometimes you will have members who will deliberately try to take advantage. One prominent pastor had one of his members suggest that he would like to render regular services from his firm on a continuing basis without charge. The pastor appreciated this courtesy and accepted it over a period of two years, whereupon he was presented a bill for all services given for the period. Though puzzled, he promptly paid the bill. However, he was not aware that this same member had given the account to the local credit union as *delinquent.* Later, the pastor was called to another church, evidently without a credit check. Still later, one of the most prestigious pulpits in the country was open to him. This pulpit committee made a routine credit check and discovered that in his record there was a notation of an unpaid bill – the two-year bill referred to above. One of the members of the pulpit committee, feeling there was surely something wrong about this report, asked an attorney to investigate. At that time the first pastorate mentioned was having problems with anonymous letters being sent to various members as a means of undermining their current pastor. Church leaders secured from the credit bureau files a photostat of the reported delinquency and found that it had been typed on the same typewriter as the anonymous letters. Law officers were called in and traced the typewriter to a man in the congregation who presumably had con- spired with the service man to smear the credit record of the preacher. His canceled check cleared the records. Some will take advantage.

Others will use gifts to the pastor as a substitute for gifts to the church and, thus, seek to buy his affection. What stance shall a pastor take? It would seem that those who want to share and have the means to share ought to be allowed to do so with appreciation and gratitude if their intentions are honorable. The gift of those who share but do not really have the means should also be accepted graciously. Perhaps the pastor could lovingly and tactfully seek to compensate in return. This is much better than rejecting a gift of the person whom you feel does not have the means to make such a gesture.

Upon assuming a pastorate, some announce their policies as to wedding fees and funeral remunerations. They will only accept expenses beyond what the church usually pays, for example, through a car allowance. Others are willing to accept a small appreciation gift. Members should not attempt to pay for service rendered but only give an expression of love between friends. However, if the pastor has announced his policy or not accepting such, he should stick to it. A pastor friend, upon being presented a gift for service rendered to one of my loved ones, returned the check to me and said, "I do not accept gifts for service rendered to one of my own." I respected him all the more highly for his consistency in attitude. Every pastor should feel and teach that the laborer is worthy of his hire. Perhaps we would do better to speak of *minister's support* instead of *minister's salary.*

The minister may have more freedom if he questions ministerial discounts. Historically, these have come from the time when preachers were paid in food and merchandise. A 10% discount to preachers was like giving 10% to the church. It was not asked for. It was simply a customary thing. But some ministers feel much better if they pay full price and tell the merchants that they prefer to do that. They may say, "The church supports us adequately. They expect me to pay my own way, and I prefer it that way. I'm grateful for your thoughtfulness and courteous consideration; but unless you normally discount such merchandise or it is something about which we may bargain in price, I prefer to pay your asking price or go elsewhere if I can get the same quality or acceptable substitute cheaper."

Use of Time

How about honesty in the use of time? *Time is the stuff that life is made of.* The minister must be a good steward of his time. As pointed out before, he has to be careful to control his time himself and not allow the members to do it.

Example: The pastor is in his study on Tuesday morning. At nine o'clock a member walks in and says, "Well, preacher, I had the day off and thought I'd come down and visit with you awhile." The pastor may just sit back as if he had all the time in the world and let the member take up his time, or he may say, "I certainly appreciate your thoughtfulness of me and am glad that you came by for an opportunity to share. I wish I could take the day off with you, but I have some things that must be done, so I can't do that. But I do have ten or fifteen minutes, so sit down and let's chat a little while." At the end of the period the pastor may arise and say, "Thank you again for coming by. Please do this a little more often," and bid the visitor goodbye.

You must recognize that sometimes when a member uses this approach, it is a means of getting in to talk about some sensitive matter, and the pastor may find himself giving the individual a little more time. For, indeed, there ought to be opportunity in the pastor's schedule for the *ministry of interruptions*. Sometimes the interruptions that we have are our biggest opportunities to minister to our people.

The pastor ought also to exercise some control over telephone time from his office. This means that when he calls a member, he will ask if it is convenient to talk at that time, for one does not have the right to barge in on another without permission. Second, he may suggest a limitation on the time. When one calls him, he may say, "I have five minutes I can spare you" or " I have an appointment in five minutes" or whatever he needs to limit the time. This may avoid small talk that takes up precious time. Again, a word of caution: There ought to be a sense of relaxation and unhurriedness in many of the activities with our people. But if one is not careful, he can *waste* a day instead of *investing* a day. My father-in-law used to say, "Too many makes too much." We can accept too many invitations, some of which simply feed our ego. We can disguise personal ambition for power and glory, and even security, for supposed enthusiasm for the Lord and evangelistic zeal.

Covetousness

Covetousness may be the preacher's most besetting sin. Only a few covet other men's wives, but some covet other ministers' churches, their buildings, their staff. Only a few covet other men's money, but they may covet other churches' members. Others covet the status of certain pulpits or even the *questionable status* of denominational positions. And some even covet degrees and titles without earning them by discipline, time and scholarship. Some covet the leisure time of the forty-hour week. Others covet the things that a more adequate salary will buy. Some covet the comforts of the more affluent. Some covet the clothes of those who dare dress in the latest styles. Some covet the authority of a business executive or the reverence given to the medical profession. Some covet the attention and companionship of political figures and the influential.

What can a minister do about his covetousness? He can be sure of his acceptance before God. He can be certain of his call. He can be confident that he is in the geography of God's will so he will not trespass on another's territory. He can recognize that honors and recognition from men are fleeting but service to God is permanent. He can really believe that a man's life does not consist in the abundance of things and that while a laborer is worthy

20

of his hire, he must recognize that society, including the church, has a distorted sense of values. Note the pay scale of the professional athlete with a college education compared with any other professional person whose training has taken him four or five years beyond college. So he, the minister, is not the only one treated unfairly because of this distorted sense of values and he should teach to correct the system without succumbing to covetousness while so doing. A minister should remember his serving role and recognize that authority of the minister grows out of respect for leadership ability and must be constantly validated by demonstration. And in respect to time, he can give up his compulsion neurosis and give priorities to the value of his own family relationships and his own health and efficiency in service to the congregation and community.

Yes, covetousness is perhaps the most common sin of all among ministers, but the fact that it is common does not make it right.

Savings and Annuity

We have not meant to imply that a minister should not plan ahead in financial matters. The oft repeated principle of *give 10%, save 10% and spend the rest gladly* may well apply. To save ten percent may be difficult, but through a carefully devised insurance program with cash accruals, the purchase of a house if a home is not furnished, and the annuity the church may provide, he may build a sizable savings. When a house is provided, some pastors try to put aside the monthly amount they would be building in equity if they were paying for their own home place. Consult a reputable financial planner about retirement plans. Be sure to consider your denominational plans, if any. Perhaps some state or national organization or foundation will add matching funds resulting in a larger retirement return.

Competency

How one relates ethically to his church family as to time may govern competence in the task. Dr. Clevis F. Horne once stated that skills alone would not make the pastor competent. He answered his question, "How do we become competent?" with six suggestions:

• *First, we must be able to say "my gospel."* The gospel does not in any way depend upon how I feel about it. The Christ event is as objective as a range of mountains but it can become a subjective reality within me. When that happens, the grace that was in Christ becomes forgiveness and healing within me. I come alive, feel living hope, and I know I have a powerful word to speak. I can then say *my gospel.* (In terms of ethical behavior, the gospel we preach by *living* among our members is the most powerful *my gospel.* J.C.H.)

• *Second, we have to lay hold of a power beyond ourselves.* The truth is that our human resources are not sufficient for our task. We so easily become exhausted before the job is done. One of the great promises made us is: there is power beyond us which is made available to us...The Holy Spirit is available to us and he gives vitality and power. We are often so weak when we could be so strong. (Ethical behavior among members involves the pastor's recognizing his boundaries and limitations as to physical strength and taking time for proper rest, recreation and leisure. J.C.H.)

• *Third, we have to believe in the importance of our work.* It is for us to believe in the importance of our work when often our culture does not. Especially is it important for us to believe in the significance of preaching... W. E. Sangster once wrote, "On his way to preach the gospel the most modest man may whisper to himself: 'Nothing more important will happen in this town this week than the work I am doing now.'" (Ethical behavior demands that we insist from our membership the right and the time for proper study that we may be strong in the pulpit. J.C.H.)

• *Fourth, we must have a healthy self-image.* The poor self-image is the undoing of many people. I believe it is the center of or a responsible factor in practically every emotional difficulty we have. Ministers are not immune to unhealthy self-images. And here is the source of much of our incompetency. How often we see ourselves as being unworthy, guilty, or inadequate.

Rather than coming to grips with our poor self-image and doing something constructive about it, we mishandle it. We seek frequently to escape the problem by accepting an image of not being really human, of being suspended somewhere between divinity and humanity. Our congregations are willing to see us that way, and we are willing frequently to be seen that way. In a sense it is a safe place. We are protected from the pain and hurt of intimacy. But if it is a safe place, it is also a lonely place. Thus the loneliness of a lot of ministers. And it is a false position. The truth is we are very human having no more divinity than any other ordinary human being. Therefore, a lot of us break under the tension between who we really are and who we appear to be.

But some of us go to the other extreme. We are too eager to let people know how human we are. We curse, tell dirty jokes, drink alcoholic beverages, and do other things in order to take the false halo from our heads. We overly expose ourselves. There is a thin line between being healthily and unhealthily human. We can so easily step over that thin line and disrobe ourselves too much. There is not only physical nudity; there is emotional nudity. And when we disrobe ourselves too much we embarrass our people and injure ourselves.

22

• *Fifth, we should have a person-centered ministry.* We must know that people are the most important realities in our churches. We are to love, care for, and serve them. They are to come first. And whenever a person really needs us, we should leave whatever we are doing – be it reading a book, preparing a sermon, or engaging in prayer and meditation – and get to that person. This kind of ministry will pay rich dividends across the years.

Here is a youth who, having passed through dangerous and turbulent years, has come upon fine manhood and says to you, "You helped me through those bad years." Here is a couple, once on the brink of separation and divorce, who are now happy again. They say to you, "Through your concern and counseling you helped save our marriage." Or here is an old person to whom you have given time and attention. And he says to you, "You have been a steadying hand during these weak years." When you hear such things, you know you would not exchange your vocation for any other, it matters not how lucrative and prestigious.

• *Sixth, there must be a place and time for renewal and replenishment.* When we keep on giving and giving with no replenishment, it is little wonder that the inner springs dry up and we feel empty and washed out. We cannot continue to give unless we receive. We cannot remain fresh unless we are replenished. Let me suggest two things.

First, we must have time for prayer, meditation, and reflection. Jesus prayed regularly and met every crisis of his life with prayer. If he couldn't get along without prayer, how can we? Yet, if we should be perfectly honest, most of us would have to confess that we are woefully inadequate here. Our *busyness* crowds out our time for prayer and meditation.

Prayer does many things. But one thing it does of greatest importance is give a vantage point from which to view life. Maybe in real prayer we come nearer seeing the world as God does than at any other time. It is as if God says, "Come stand beside me and see the world as I see it."

If prayer allows us in some sense to stand beside God, it also allows us to stand beside our fellows. Real social sensitivity is born of prayer. We become aware of the pain and hope, suffering and longing, of those caught up in this pilgrimage with us.

Prayer makes us aware of the world of spiritual and intangible reality without which our lives cannot be fulfilled. Great power is laid within our reach.

Second, we need a retreat for sharing and study. We need to read good books, meet great minds, and share with others who are on a journey of truth. If we don't, we will be like the preacher of whom one of his members said, "My pastor can dive the deepest, stay the longest, and come up the driest of any man I have ever known."

Personal Devotions

I cannot really add to what Chevis Horne has said, but in conversation with many ministers through the years I have been led to believe that during the early years of Christian experience most ministers found it both necessary and profitable to continue a *methodical method* of daily Bible reading and prayer. Others have found it possible to change their techniques in this respect. But all agree that when they neglect their personal devotions, they find their wellsprings of creativity drying up. They find it necessary to go to the Bible for more than just a text of scripture for next Sunday's sermon and find it necessary to pray concerning themselves, their own needs and those of their people. As has been said, one should talk to God about men before he goes to talk to men about God. Indeed, it is rather hypocritical for a pastor to encourage his congregation to have times of personal devotion and family prayer when he does not practice such himself.

Some ministers have told me that they pray as they walk, getting spiritual exercise at the same time they get physical exercise. Others say they pray as they drive their car, but most seem to feel the need of some time alone and apart without distractions. Many indicate that their best time is early in the morning. Others find that it has never been quite right for them to set a specific period, while some feel that in a sense they are always living in an attitude of prayer, practicing the admonition to pray without ceasing.

Many ministers find it not only helpful to read the Bible devotionally and pray but also to read poetry, hymns and other inspirational type reading (other than sermons) that really help them feel some thrust toward spiritual growth. Occasionally there are books or sermons that do this, but psychologically, ministers find it difficult to read books of sermons for inspiration because we are too homiletical or sermon-conscious ourselves.

If the minister is going to continue to have flow up in him the wells of living water that he may have refreshment for himself and for others, he must keep the wellsprings unclogged that the power of God may flow through him as well as be felt in him.

What about Plagiarism?

One pastor who was always telling his members how hard he was working in his study was known to preach verbatim sermons from books, Billy Graham and others, without any credit to the author even for the ideas expressed. One would find it almost impossible to give credit for all the ideas he has that might be planted away in the subconscious to surface later, but without credit he should certainly not take the position: "When better sermons are printed, I will preach them."

People respect the man who may preface his sermon material by saying: "In my reading, I was impressed by _____." "According to Dr. _____." "There were a number of sources for my message today, among them a very excellent book by _____." "No doubt I have been influenced by the writings of _____ as I prepared this message for I'm very much indebted to him for the help he has given me in understanding these passages of scripture."

While one would not expect a minister to be a scrupulous perfectionist in giving credit, he would not want him to be a plagiarist by constantly using others' ideas without some acknowledgement of his source.

Borrowing and Lending Books or Tapes

If the minister is a borrower, he should return borrowed items as he has promised. Careful records should be kept by the lender and he should not hesitate to notify the borrower when the return is past due.

With the widespread use of copying machines, one also must be careful about violation of copyrights. While it would be a technical violation, most ministers would not feel that they have ethically violated a copyright if they photostat a paragraph to quote, with credit, in the Sunday morning message. But to copy a tape that is specifically copyrighted or to copy and sell another person's material such as music for a choir production or to make use of it for that matter, is certainly a violation of copyrighted material and according to law, this is as much stealing as if you seized another's property for your own use.

Dealing with Sexual Attractions

The Problem Clergymen Don't Talk About is the title of a book by Charles Rassier of the Institute of Pastor Care, Harrisburg, Pennsylvania. Published by Westminster Press in 1976, it deals pointedly, theologically and psychologically with the problem pastors sometimes have in dealing with a female church member toward whom they may have a sexual attraction. Indeed, it is a problem that most preachers don't talk about except in gossip about other ministers who have had *female trouble*.

Some treat the problem by denying that it ever is one with them. Others avoid any close association such as in counseling, ministering to the grief stricken except in a very casual way, and visiting lost or ill women in a cold professional manner.

Early in his ministry a clergyman usually receives such warnings as "Watch out for women." "Keep your hands off women." "See women only when your wife is with you." "Never have an appointment with a woman unless someone else is around." "Be careful about frequencies of visits to widows." "Be careful about being in the car with a woman." As a result, some young men look upon women as seducers and evil – as daughters of Eve. They seem to forget Adam's responsibility. Others fear women and want *to keep them in their place*. Still others realize that there are certain dynamics in any interpersonal relationship that may create feelings or impulses that may need special concern. There are those who are very fearful, embarrassed or guilt-ridden by sexual feelings that may be aroused. These persons fail to differentiate between temptation and sin. Or between feelings and behavior. One can recognize a feeling, even a mutual feeling, without exploiting it. It should be said with emphasis that *it can happen to any of us.*

How well one is acquainted with himself, his feelings, his ability to maintain self-respect as well as respect for others – all these factors enter into the vulnerable nature of the pastoral relationship. Sometimes dependencies exist or are created. Advice is sought. Maybe an authority figure, a father figure, is needed. This caters to the *need to be needed*, which is appropriate.

This is certainly not the place to treat adequately such a serious and common problem. We are simply pointing out that if the pastor behaves prudently, he will honestly face his own feelings and assume responsibility for his emotional responses to his parishioners. He will learn to know the gender joys with their overtones of sexuality without violating socially or morally acceptable behavior patterns.

Certainly one does his best with his people when he helps them as one human being to another. That is, he divests himself of any aura of the angelic and recognizes the treasure he has to give is in an earthen vessel. But as a shepherd-priest, he can still communicate the highest and best of which he is capable. Therefore, he must understand what is going on in the interchange. He does, hopefully, consider his reputation, but should it be weighed more heavily than the reputation of the other? Does it seem advisable to set limits as to how the relationship is to continue – the place, time of day and length of time? He may suggest his availability by phone in times of undue stress, but he will be more respected if he keeps these calls to a minimum and for a reasonable length of time and observes common courtesy with the rest of his own family.

Sometimes temporary transference is made from some previous significant person. This could have some degree of hostility. But in the context of this discussion, it is more apt to be admiration, adulation, dependence, clinging, et al. A direct avowal of love may be heard and interpreted, "I'd do anything for you." How to deal with this without panic or rejection or ignoring it becomes a real art – but it *can* be learned. The pastor might respond as follows:

"You honor me by expressing your confidence in my integrity. You believe I will not exploit your feelings. I respect you all the more for this. We each have commitments that preclude any behavior contrary to the trust you have expressed. Thank you for your expression of love and affirmation of me as a person."

He might add, "In relationships such as we share, it follows that we should develop a high degree of caring for each other."

Or, "You also are much loved, and I would affirm you as a person of tremendous worth and concern. I, too, would express confidence in your integrity and your ability to handle your feelings in ways that will not embarrass either of us now or later."

One should pray as he handles delicate feelings discreetly and tenderly without physical involvement that he will later regret. The mature pastor will not be embarrassed to seek help at this point from another professional.

On Sheep Stealing

The practice of some ministers to proselyte members of other churches or denominations is universally condemned. Some ministers justify it for themselves and condemn it in others. In our urban society, with people constantly changing churches, it might be difficult to always confer with the pastor whose member is leaving to join one's congregation, but if at all possible, this would be the courteous and ethical thing to do. The pastor receiving the member should explain the circumstances as they have been explained to him and give the other pastor opportunity to tell him what he knows about the person or family.

Suppose the member is not in good standing? In the Baptist faith we grant letters of members *of good standing* to congregations. Questions on what motivates a member to leave are just as important as what motivates him to join another congregation. While most of us would prefer that families be united in the church and most families prefer to be a part of the same church group, there are circumstances in which they are divided by denominational ties. This ought to be a matter for the family to work out and not one in which the pastor intervenes or interferes except as he may be invited, else he may set up a conflict within the family.

The minister should be on guard when he has occasion to visit in homes of those belonging to other denominations or church congregations. Sometimes these are social experiences, business relationships or maybe death in the family or wedding attendance. Some ministers feel that they can proselyte in jest, but such overtures are often taken seriously by the member who may brag to his pastor or fellow church member that he has been invited to join Dr. _____'s congregation.

Most ministers are rightly concerned about building up their own congregation in numbers as well as in faith; but the pastor should also exercise concern about how other ministers look upon him and especially how he may appear before the Lord in his motivation to build up the congregation. Certainly we are not edifying the body of Christ if we are building up one congregation by tearing down another.

The Pastor and Discretionary Funds

Some churches furnish the pastor with funds to be used at his discretion in meeting benevolent needs of the congregation or community. Even though these records are not publicized, the pastor should keep adequate records of funds disbursed – to whom and for what. In event any question is raised by some concerned member, he will have records to justify payments from the fund.

When On an Expense Account

Churches have different expectations of pastors who attend conventions, conferences and similar meetings on expense accounts. Some set up a lump sum which the pastor may spend at his discretion without accounting. Others have a *draw account* up to a certain amount. Some simply try to make an estimate for the necessary items and expect the pastor to use his judgment as to keeping near the budget figure. It is wise to have a clear understanding of what is expected or acceptable to the church.

It costs only a little more to go first class is a popular expression, and some churches would be disappointed in their pastor if he did not travel comfortably and eat well. Others would feel the minister should be more careful with *their money.*

Pastors are sometimes invited to represent certain denominational agencies or departments or otherwise travel on denominational expense accounts. For 24 years of my pastoral ministry I had this privilege. I asked one denominational executive how I should handle the expense account. He replied, "Get every penny that is coming to you and not one cent more." I have found this to be very good counsel. The pastor who thus travels will find this well nigh impossible, especially if he is asked to use his personal automobile in travel, as seldom do mileage rates compensate for the cost, but it is a *good head rule.*

Some people splurge on expense accounts, eating expensive meals and such. Sometimes it seems advisable to eat better than at other times. Circumstances and appetite are both to be considered. My own *head rule* is to order as though I were paying the bill myself unless I have been instructed to do otherwise. One time this will mean a sandwich or a bowl of soup; another time, a cafeteria meal; once in a while, a steak or specialty of the area. When all of these factors are considered, one can feel he is spending judiciously.

I do not think it wise to sit up all night to keep from paying room rent. I agree with what Dr. Chester Quarles, my one time Executive Secretary, said when we were both very fatigued and still had a night meeting and a very long drive. I suggested that we stop, get a room, and try to sleep about four hours. He said, "Good boy! It is just as important to care for the Lord's man as it is to take care of the Lord's money." The ethical pastor will find the balance between stewardship of energy and money as he travels on an expense account.

Use of Tobacco as an Illustration
of Factors in Ethical Decision Making

In certain sections of the country some ministers use tobacco; in other communities this is a no-no! Suppose he does not use tobacco but does not feel it is a moral issue. He still may have a sign in his office saying, "Thank You for Not Smoking." And it should be permissible for him to suggest that someone not smoke in his automobile or in his home if he prefers. On the other hand, the church may have a rule against smoking in the church building and the pastor may have a counselee who is a nicotine addict and cannot stay in a room longer than fifteen minutes without a cigarette and asks permission to smoke. The pastor may plead the church rule or he may grant permission on the basis of seeking to help the individual through his emotional dilemma.

What about the minister's own use of tobacco? Several factors should be considered. He may consider his health or be concerned about his influence. He may not use it often enough to be any special health hazard for him (from his point of view). He may be in a community where the customs, habits and manners do not question his use of tobacco. Yet he may have to face all these issues. Paul stated the principle in I Cor. 6:12: "All things are lawful unto me but all things are not expedient." The term "expediency" may apply. For instance, my father was a heavy smoker. As a child growing up, my view of comfort was to see him in a rocking chair before the fire with his pipe. No doubt this mental image influenced my use of tobacco for a time. I liked the taste. I used to like the smell. Now I sit in "No Smoking" sections and what was once a fragrance is now an odor in most instances. Why the change? I began to think about the money being spent and my stewardship of material things. But the biggest reason was the attitude of my

10-year-old son who took occasion to tear up my cigarettes as I once wanted to empty Dad's whiskey bottle. I began to understand something of the emotional trauma that he had since he felt I was perhaps committing suicide by using cigarettes. I was determined not to smoke for his sake. However, I do not feel superior to those who follow the tobacco road. I believe it is ethical for me to encourage those who have not started to refrain from smoking and also to try to help those who would like to stop. I have in my office a sign that says, "Thank You for Not Smoking," but I also have a ashtray that I can pull out for those who ask permission to smoke.

Use of Vulgarisms

The principle of expediency may further apply in other types of social situations. The pastor operating in the liberty that he has in Christ may feel that he is free and that he cannot give away his Christian liberty by yielding to other people and their opinions as to what is right and what is wrong for him. An esteemed college English professor once said, "Use slang if slang at the moment expresses best what you desire to say." This admonition may be correct except for many occasions in the pulpit. Vulgarity and obscenities are always out of place for the minister, and it is never appropriate to use the name of the Lord in vain. Some find themselves saying, "My Lord" or "My God," in ways that to the bystander sound like profanity, though someone knowing the individual realizes that he has no intention of being profane. Such speech patterns are simply not expedient for the minister regardless of his motivation. Profanities and vulgarities are becoming such a part of American speech patterns that studious attention must be used to guard against it. The point is people expect something better than that from a minister! As Lloyd C. Douglas once said, "The people make a priest out him whether he likes it or not." If the minister tells an off-color story or uses vulgarity or profanity in the presence of his members, they will often quote such to others and say, "The preacher told it, so I guess it's all right for me to tell it." There is a difference in cleverness and humor in the use of words and vulgarity, but the line is very thin.

Avoiding Gossip about Yourself

The pastor should seek to avoid situations that would be conducive to gossip; but this is not always possible. One remembers the counsel of George W. Truett: "Never take counsel of your fears or appearances, but do your whole duty and then unfalteringly leave the results with God."

When one is a newcomer to the community, he has to be much more careful. After becoming well known, the need to be on guard against gossip will lessen as people will not be quite so prone to ascribe impure motives to his activities.

Frequent visits to a woman in her home in the absence of her husband should be avoided, assuming that she is alone. If repeated conferences are necessary, it is much better for her to come to the church office where the secretary is near by.

It is very difficult to control gossip or to call back a story once it is given, so a minister is rightly concerned if gossip includes him. However, his good reputation will usually overcome it, especially if he will inform a few trusted leaders of the facts. They, in turn, are often able to handle untrue stories being repeated.

On Keeping Appointments

What about the ethics of appointment keeping? A pastor should keep his appointments promptly. He has no right to impose upon the time of others just because he is the pastor. There are emergencies, of course, but when there are, the other person should be notified as soon as possible. Consideration of others is certainly a mark of gentlemanly conduct.

Last minute telephone interruptions often keep ministers from being punctual in their appointments. It is ethical to explain to the calling person that you have an appointment and will have to leave but will call back at a designated time. Telephone calls should not take priority just because you are the one *for whom the bell tolls.* Prior commitments must be honored.

Obeying the Law

There is another hazard at this point – the hazard of hurry. The mental picture that many have of their pastor is his being harried – always in a hurry and breaking the speed laws. Some pastors disobey traffic laws and brag about it. The fact that officers are sometimes lenient with the preacher who has a emergency is no excuse for him to set such a poor example in obedience to the law. For whatever rationalization a man may have for disobeying the law, if he is caught he should surely pay his fine and not accept a traffic ticket fix unless there are extenuating circumstances that he and the judge both recognize as being valid. While most of us would not think of violation of traffic laws as having earth-shaking moral significance, there is a sense in which, if it becomes a habit pattern, it may reflect something of one's regard for the law and government in general. When there are exceptions made for the minister as to law, such as jury duty in most states, he should not feel that this makes him above the law but should note that the exceptions are made that he might better serve the people. In event there should be criticism by some unthinking member, then the proper rationale of the law-makers should be explained. Some areas where this may be necessary, for example, are housing allowance, car allowance, and other professional expense for ministers that are considered *tax exempt*.

The Questionable Ethics of the Unopened Letter

It is unfortunate that some ministers brag about not having time to open their mail. These same ministers are generally most discourteous about answering their mail. Surely the person whose very life and ministry depends upon good communication practices should find time to daily read his mail and promptly answer. Others are inconvenienced by a pastor's procrastination in this regard.

In responding to invitations, he should not convey the impression that he is waiting for something better to come along. If this is actually the case, he should just politely refuse the invitation and forget about it. While there is a tendency toward simplicity, directness, and even bluntness in letter writing in our day, the words please and thank you are just as much in order in letter writing as they are in personal conversation. A minister should never feel that he is above common courtesy in communication.

Some ministers are so arrogant they think that they should be able to make requests without courtesy or accept favors without a simple *thank you* or a similar expression of gratitude.

If one has a secretary, he may request that she acknowledge receipt of a letter in his absence, suggesting to the correspondent that the letter will be brought to the pastor's attention upon his return. The habit of giving prompt attention to mail also assures that bills may be paid promptly.

"I'm sorry, honey, Daddy doesn't have time to talk to you just now. He's writing a book on family togetherness."

"YES, SON—THE PASTOR AND I ARE FRIENDS.   WHY DO YOU ASK?"

"WELL, AFTER LISTENING TO YOU AND MOM TALK—I WAS JUST WONDERING."

4.
THE MINISTER AND
THE CHURCH MEMBERS

Dr. Charles E. Jefferson writes in *The Ministering Shepherd*, "Often the hungry sheep look up and are not fed." The pastor must love, guide, guard and warn the sheep in his shepherd ministry. He doesn't know how to feed them properly if he doesn't know *their needs*.

Pastors use all sorts of visitation methods to get acquainted with their membership. I often wondered how W. F. Powell, long-time pastor of the First Baptist Church of Nashville, kept up so well for so many years with such a large membership. I learned from one of his members that during the week following the time when the persons presented themselves for membership, Dr. Powell camped on their trail. He showed up in their home at least once and made some provision to get acquainted in a special way with the husband or another member of the family in order to learn about the family talents, background, capabilities, and something of their interests and concerns. By the end of the week, he would ask some other person or family whom he thought would be congenial to sponsor them for involvement in the life of the church. Then the next week he "took off" after the new members who joined that Sunday. Dr. Powell did some prospect visitation but most of his visitation, so I was told, was to cultivate the new members. He counted on this kind of rapport and fellowship to be contagious with the new members so that they would encourage others to attend First Baptist Church.

Charles Tope when pastor of Northwest Hills Baptist Church, Oklahoma City, used the combination of visitation and praying for the membership by name. He literally prays over the church roll in a systematic way, letting the people know that is he praying for them at a certain time. He calls them by telephone to say, "I have prayed for you today," or, "I am praying for you today and wonder if you have special needs." If he cannot reach them by phone, he writes that he did remember them in prayer on this particular day. This kind of prayerful pastoral concern has deepened the relationship between pastor and members.

Respecting Differences
All church members should be treated with respect regardless of their background, prior spiritual condition (with reference to kinds of sins peculiar to them), education, wealth, culture, race, sex, age, physical handicaps, or whatever. There should be respect for differences, including differences in

35

opinion – especially when their opinion differs from that of the minister. The minister ought to try to like everybody. This is most difficult for many to do. I used to ask, "What is it in that person that causes me not to like him?" Perhaps better, I should ask, "What is it in me that causes me not to like him?"

One technique of dealing with personality conflicts is to pray for the other person as well as yourself concerning your relationship and try to get better acquainted with the person whom you have a tendency to dislike. The pastor should be careful of *cronyism*. Still, he should try to be a friend to the leader of all the *cliques* of the church. I used the word clique to refer to small groups of which all churches are composed. It's impossible for members to feel close to *all* other members of the church, and they feel a part and a sense of belonging if they feel accepted by a small group – which may be a Sunday School class, women's group, men's group, choir or some social group within the church.

No Power Plays!

Two curses that a pastor should avoid are *power plays* and *manipulation*. It is easy for a pastor to manipulate because he is the authority figure. It is easy for him to use the chairmen of committees and other groups to manipulate to his own ends and not let the church *be the church* in the sense of being a democratic institution. He may be tempted to use some influential member in power plays, but more likely he is tempted to use his own influence to demonstrate his power. Whoever originally said *power corrupts* was not referring just to politicians. This can be true of pastors or a denominational leader. While Jesus was *all power*, He diffuses that power through the Holy Spirit among the members and that combination in the community makes an effective witness.

The pastor by virtue of his training, experience and study may indeed know what is best for his congregation. Yet others may have some good ideas, too. An informed membership will respond to good leadership, but people generally resent any pastor or church committee or group of deacons who tries to run rough-shod over the congregation.

It is well for the pastor to give suggestions to church committees and to committee chairmen in terms of agenda for consideration, but the wise and busy pastor will delegate some responsibility for making and implementing decisions. Responsibility always carries with it accountability; and if a committee or church as a whole makes a decision, it thus becomes responsible for it and is accountable. So the pastor does not need to feel the full weight of the project being completed. Respect for opinions and respect for differences must be foremost.

Stewardship of Time – Again!

Some ministers give an undue amount of time to administrative tasks that ought to be delegated to members for the sake of building them up in the body of Christ. Here are some more suggestions without discussion concerning *behavior patterns* in the stewardship of time.

1. Do not attempt too much. Your timetable may become too tight.

2. Invest your day – don't spend it. Use your phone more and your legs less.

3. Plan your work, but don't substitute puttering for planning.

4. Budget and balance your time. Be careful about too much long-range planning that ignores immediate needs. Be careful about follow-through. Finish what you start. Pastors should be careful about planning and promotion. Often we feel that our church members know so much more than they do and our plans take too much for granted.

5. Leave some blank spaces on your calendar pad. Allow for interruptions.

Keep Your Promotion Ethical

A Texas pastor, Bill Austin, wrote an article entitled "Keep Your Promotion Ethical" in which he suggested three key standards by which promotion ethics could be checked. They are as follows:

1. *Promotion must not intimidate.* To employ the pressures of intimidation and embarrassment is the lowest form of promotion. To suggest that one is disloyal or uncooperative or unspiritual because he does not get on the bandwagon is appealing to the basic desire for acceptance.

One might want to take a look at slogans used in campaign promotions. They may suggest that those who do not participate are considered disloyal and dishonorable. Question: Are the results of the campaign worth alienating precious personalities who feel that you consider them disloyal – the worst thing you can say of a man?

2. *Promotion must not assume Divine authority.* We should not declare that "God expects you to do this" or "God will be grieved if you do not give." "Jesus wants every member to enlist." "The Lord gave me this program." In our obsession to succeed we are on very dangerous grounds if we become victims of the Messiah complex. We also increase the weight of guilt and destroy many useful people who go through life feeling condemned because they did not do God's will – that is, participate in this latest fad or promotional method.

3. *Promotion must not presume or misplace total commitment.* All grandiose themes tend to do this. We must be careful that we do not

mislead our people into thinking that attending every service for six or seven weeks automatically will crown Him Lord – nor does a concerted visitation effort of limited duration necessarily prove love. Most such promotions involve calling upon bigger words and more poetic slogans the next time. We use cliches and keep applying them to restricted and sometimes trivial campaigns. Then when we want to use the same terminology in a really great appeal for some fuller life commitment, we have already undercut the effectiveness of the slogan. The minister does not need to appeal to the reactionary forces of guilt complexes, fear or rejection and emotional instability. We can take our people higher with us as we increase the moral tone of our promotional schemes, thereby increasing the quality of the desire to participate.

To inspire greater quality of desire we must respect the intelligence of our people and give a clear description of our intentions and our anticipated results. We should state the real purpose of the promotion and give it a name if it needs one that is self-explanatory, honest and relevant to the issue; and when we do this, we may be surprised how quickly the church members will respond to a truthful, factual appeal rather than a glamorous, emotional gimmick. Those who at this time cannot participate will not feel intimidated or ostracized, and we'll feel much better because we have used integrity in our promotional efforts.

The Principle of Involvement

The principle of involvement may be centered around the text, "And there went with him a band of men whose heart God had touched." They went not *for* Him and not *to* Him, but they gathered *around* Him. Perhaps a bigger error in modern day church life is to mistake activity, meetings and attendance for involvement. The member as a volunteer worker is important, but people are not expendable to the program. To involve people in *their* program takes more time, but it makes up time in the end. This involvement considers their stewardship of experience, the stewardship of opportunity and respect for their ideas as you face the opportunity in light of the experience of the members. They respond with responsibility and accountability. The principle of involvement may consider the psychology in the generation of ideas. Crudely put, it is "have the idea but generate it in the church member so that it becomes *his* instead of just yours."

The spirit of leadership, therefore, is the leadership of the Spirit. The law of leadership is the law of love. We are not to be ignorant of our fellow workers but respect and honor those in other tasks in the life of the church. New Testament church leadership takes a genuine interest in people. When Jesus saw the multitudes, He was moved with compassion. We have a tendency to count the people. He identified with the people.

Pastoral programming considers the activities and curriculum on the basis of determined spiritual needs of the people. Such programming considers the past history of the church and the spiritual development of the membership to this point. Such programming acknowledges that the church is to be a force in the community and vitally related to it.

The Principle of Organization

The New Testament pattern of church organization was "as a need arose, they organized to meet the need." But we must be sure that we *have a need*. This also should take into consideration our boundaries, our limitations and the limitations of our people. Many ministers try to promote too much. If it takes all of our energies to keep an organization going, we have too much organization. We may need less organization to do more effective work. We may find that we can get along without some prescribed office or committee. The minister is not called to promote organizations but to meet the needs of the people. For example, if you have no leadership, you should abolish the organization; if you don't have a teacher you don't have a class. There is no such thing as a class without a teacher. You may have a group of boys learning the wrong things in a good environment, but they are not going to be more spiritual because they have absorbed something from the veneer of the pew or the splinter from the chair.

The *organization man syndrome* attacks many churches in spite of the pastor. We can waste much time and energy comparing ourselves with ourselves or with others. We can also get into the paralysis of analysis, the deadening of perpetual diagnosis of our situation. Some results are measurable, and some results are discernible; but primarily, we are not called to be successful. We are not called to make an impression. We are not called even to do a job. We are called to give our witness for Christ.

Always there is too much to do. But as we go about the frustrating task of realizing our seeming insignificance, we do recall that we are created for a purpose. Someone has well said, "The way to be great is to find out what God is doing and then join Him." To paraphrase: The way to develop an effective church program is to follow scriptural principles and allow God to lead us in that path of greatness that comes from loving service to Him who has called us.

Seek Fruit Bearing

The minister in a church program must be very careful of his priorities and seek to be alert that all the needs of the church family are met. This involves staff, either paid or volunteer. For example, the music leader can only do his part, but the church program must include those who are not gifted or are not interested in music, and he ought to be the first to insist on this. Surely the pastor would insist on it. The same thing is true of other activities or programs of the church. Keep in mind the objective "to edify the whole body of Christ."

There are some types of church leaders the minister works around – avoids, contends with, or seeks to change. They are:

1. Those who love the pre-eminence – as Diotrephes (3 John: 9).
2. Those who love the things of this world – as Demos (2 Timothy 4:10).
3. Those who want to buy power – as Simon (Acts 8:18).
4. Those who are indifferent – as Gallio, who cared for none of these things (Acts 18:17).
5. Those who work only when convenient – as Apollos (1 Cor. 16:12).
6. Those who teach false doctrine and cause division (Romans 16:17).

Much of the minister's work is in the realm of encouragement. This does not involve a Pollyanna sort of backslapping but genuine affirmation of the abilities and achievements of the members as the minister watches their spiritual growth. The minister must be concerned that the members bear fruit:

– the fruit of character (Gal. 5:22).
– the fruit of consecration – fruit, more fruit, much fruit (John 15).
– the fruit of cooperation (1 Cor. 3:6-9).

Teach Cooperation

In the light of what has been said above, it is easy to understand that the pastor has obligations toward his members, not toward conformity but in cooperation. The purpose of cooperation in the church family is defined in Ephesians 4:11-16. It might be stated as "for the immediate equipment of God's people, for work of service, for the ultimate building up of the body of Christ, to obtain unity in the faith, to a knowledge of Christ, to mature manhood *growing up in a perfect union with Christ*, to avoid new methods of error, and growing of the body of Christ for its building up in love." Cooperation is an inescapable necessity. It is essential to our common interest. What benefits one helps all; what hinders one hurts all. The pastor should teach cooperation as a biblical principle, actually beginning in the Genesis story of creation and running like a thread through the entire Bible.

A pastor must not be derelict in teaching cooperation in the great missionary enterprise. We have much precedent for this in the scriptures: sending out missionaries (Acts 13:1ff); concerning problems of common interest (Acts 15:1-29); administering missionary funds (Acts 20:4, Romans 15:25-27, I Cor. 16:14, II Cor. 8:1-9, 15).

In denominational life the regional, state convention, and the national convention are areas of cooperation for the churches. All churches are on the same level. We have channels of cooperation from the churches and channels of promotion for the denomination. But the program in each area is a program of those churches desiring to voluntarily cooperate.

Most churches will have the desire to cooperate with each other in missionary enterprise when the members are informed about the denominational activity beyond their own church. So the minister has an ethical obligation to teach the New Testament principles of missions and see to it that the church life curriculum includes the story of the expansion of Christianity and that there are those who are informed about what missionaries do in the various fields, who and where they are. He should thrill the members with some of the results of missions for most of us are directly obligated to some missionary for hearing the gospel ourselves. Therefore, obligation is upon every Christian to accept the missionary passion of the church as outlined by Christ.

Special Attention to the Aging, Children and Youth

It would seem that the pastor should give special attention to each member of his congregation, but there is a unique sense in which attention should be given to the aging, youth and children. There should be warmth, respect for personality and attempts to build self-esteem in the person to whom you are directing your attention. Often children are overlooked, and the aging are neglected. It is sometimes thought that young people do not desire attention as they are seeking to pull away from adults and toward their peer group. But experience indicates that youth will always welcome the pastor's personal attention, especially if it is given in private. It is unfortunate, indeed, when any one of these three groups of folk feel that the pastor is above giving them attention or is not considerate of their needs. Many older people never feel the touch of another human being who cares for them except as they shake hands with the pastor or he gives them an affectionate hug around the shoulder. Some older people have told me that this attention from the pastor is what keeps them going from week to week.

It is said that children and dogs can spot a phony. It is well for a pastor to get down on a child's level when talking to him. Some find it convenient to drop down on one knee when being introduced to a small child. Others, like Jesus, take little children up in their arms and bless them by a tender, affectionate concern. Many find that little children want to be sure to get their "hug from the preacher" before they go home. This kind of personal attention is much better than the candy jar on the pastor's desk. But either may be a means of winning their attention and consequently their affection.

Treatment of Singles

Not yet married singles are often ignored or neglected. If attention is given, it is in the nature of a *put-down*. For example: "Why isn't a nice girl like you married?" Many equate wholeness with marriage, but our wholeness is derived by our being created in the image of God. Singles should not be treated as half-persons or inferior persons. The failure to provide for them organizationally or to use them in church life is a subtle way of saying, "You don't count as much as the others." "You are not important to us." "There are only a few of you, so it doesn't matter much." The shepherd ministry will use all the creativity of which he is capable to say, "You count!" "I care." "You are important to us."

Formerly married singles are among the untouchables we discuss in chapter five.

How Does a Minister Deal with Malpractices of Church Members?

Malpractice could cover a multitude of sins. It could involve matters of dishonesty in business dealings; conducting businesses that are in disrepute in the community, such as selling pornography or liquor; or gambling. The fundamental question is: How can one act redemptively toward such a church member?

"Brethren, if a man be overtaken in a fault, ye which are spiritual restore such an one in a spirit of meekness; considering thyself, lest thou also be tempted" (Gal. 6:1).

Suppose a man becomes a Christian and he is engaged in some unsavory business. The pastor's attitude could well be: "If the Lord tells you to give up your business, you should do it. If he wants you to give it up, I'm sure he has something else for you to do. So why not pray about it and look for the possibility of some other job?" I've seen this happen on several occasions in a very productive way without the church member feeling undue guilt or staying in a position detrimental to his reputation as a new Christian or to the church.

42

The ministry of restoration is probably one of the most difficult ministries of all. It is much easier for a person to say as they said of Judas, "He went out from us because he was not of us."

Gossip as Malpractice

One of the most difficult things to handle is gossip. The pastor himself must be very careful not to gossip about church members. He must not carry emotional germs from one person to another or from one family to another. Instead of being a bearer of glad tidings, some pastors are bearers of bad tidings. When words of gossip are brought to a minister, he ought to be careful about believing the story and exceedingly careful in his response to the one bringing it. He may find that the individual may tell *him* something and then go out and quote the conversation as though the minister said it. Or the gossiper may be wanting an ally in some conflict that he is having with another member. One tactic is to face the person with whatever reason he may have for repeating the story. One response might be: "If things are like you say they are, this person surely needs our love and understanding. Let's get on our knees and pray for him right now."

One man recalls that shortly after going to a pastorate he received a telephone call for an appointment with a prominent woman of the city who was a member of another denomination. She came and sought to poison the pastor's mind concerning one of his church members. The pastor's response was just as we have stated: "If the situation is as bad as you say it is, this person surely needs our love and understanding, so let's get down on our knees and pray for this person." The proud socialite got on her knees, and the pastor asked her to audibly pray for the person about whom she had been gossiping. It was not long before she made a hasty exit, and the matter was never approached again.

If it is necessary to get at the facts, one should go in love to the persons involved. Do not act alone. Two persons who are obviously friends of the one whom you are approaching might go together. Careful attention should be given to whether or not value can be derived from confronting the gossiper, and one must be careful in evaluating whether the one being gossiped about should know. It could be that the pastor could make himself available in such a way that the member will indicate to him that he knows he is being talked about and thus give the pastor opportunity to be helpful.

5.

THE MINISTER IN WORSHIP
AND FELLOWSHIP

An eight-year-old boy who was being bused out of his neighborhood to a church several miles away said to his neighbor, "At church Sunday our pastor swallowed a worm! What did you do at your church?"

The neighbor replied, "Well, we studied the Bible and worshiped God!"

"Is that all?!" exclaimed the boy.

Such antics are a travesty on worship and dishonor God. Some men turn the pulpit into an entertainment center and prostitute worship to sensationalism.

Indeed, public worship has been neglected in many churches. Because it is so often poorly done, the pastor may need to seek immediate and prompt improvement in the worship experience. People increasingly need the rich religious experience of worship as life continues to grow more tense, exacting and complex.

It is unethical to stress *preaching attendance* as synonymous with worship. Since there is not much emphasis in seminaries on worship, pastors often are not well trained to lead in public worship. Many have an order of service and hold opening exercises or devotionals as substitutes. In your tradition, there may be some aversion to certain liturgical forms, but the task of the modern church leader who would rescue Christian worship from the tragic depths to which it has fallen becomes apparent when we understand the historic development through which Christian architecture, art and liturgy have passed. The pastor should feel free to claim and use the best of all ages – that is, the best that is in keeping with our interpretation of the biblical forms of worship.

Hindrances to Worship

Worship often fails in its lack of impressiveness and solemnity, in the poverty of material used, in its lack of unity, in its musical short- comings, and particularly in the non-participation of the congregation. There are some things that hinder public worship, most of which can be corrected tactfully by the minister's leadership, such as:

1. Use of the auditorium for too many activities.

2. General clutter, especially around the pulpit.

3. Lack of planning an order of worship. Many would desire to keep a certain amount of informality in the service.

4. Lack of order when it is planned. This is not to suggest that changes

should not be made after plans have been carefully laid. As one black pastor said, "If I want to change the order of the service, I do it. You see, I'm the pastor of the bulletin. If doesn't tell me what to do; I tell it what to do." And certainly there should be leeway for that. But there can be order even in an extemporaneous way.

It is not ethical for the pastor to call people to worship and not plan for it. Many plan well for their sermon preparation, but they do not plan much for the worship service or for their role as a leader.

Public worship should be reverent, inspiring, intelligent and restful. We need to give more attention to the house of worship, the sanctuary – *dedicated place*. The pastor should plan with the one in charge of music. There should be synchronization as to theme and progression.

The minister should give special attention to the place of the Bible reading, which may involve practice in reading the scriptures as well as the proper choice of devotional reading. Those who follow the Lectionary have fewer problems at this point.

Prayer in Worship

Prayer is the soul of Christian worship. Public prayer is the hardest task of the public service. The pastoral prayer should be thought through. The words should be simple. It should be an attempt to unite all hearts in the prayer experience with some premeditative order. One should not preach in prayer and should not be routine or conventional. Prayer should be full of Christian tenderness, recognizing help of the Holy Spirit as one prays.

Music and Worship

Music usually takes up about one-third of the time the congregation spends in worship. Sometimes, more! Often several hymns are listed but only a few verses of each is sung as the music leader takes up more time talking about the hymns or introducing them than in the singing. I have clocked this several times to prove that this is so. You say I should have been worshiping? I wanted to – badly. But he was *distracting* me rather than using the music to *lead* me in worship. As one once prayed, "God deliver us from a talking singer and a singing preacher." I have told evangelistic singers privately, "You take care of the singing and let me take care of the preaching." This is not to infer that ministers who have musical talent should not use it in special numbers. And sometimes brief transition statements of hymn stories are appropriate.

A beautiful special number just before the minister brings the message both prepares the congregation and inspires the preacher. Music, properly planned and interwoven appropriately with reverent movement, adds immeasurably to worship. When the movement of the service is slowed by comments of the music leader, the worshipful response is more often hindered than helped.

The minister has an obligation to the congregation, to his music leadership and to himself to see that the music is kept in balance with the other elements in the worship experience. Therefore, he has the right to both suggest and demand changes that would, in his opinion, improve the worship. He should be careful in so doing not to impose personal preference as to types of music but allow for balance or other preferences as long as they are in keeping with the feeling range of worship of his congregation. If he thinks their taste should be improved, he should work with the music director to gradually bring about this change.

Should the minister join in the singing of hymn? Certainly, if he can carry a tune but maybe not so lustily as to call attention to himself. He should be careful, too, if he is near a microphone and exercise more care if the worship service is broadcast.

Music can well be the language of the Spirit. It can be a most valuable medium of worship.

Announcements

Where, oh where, to put them? How to shorten them? Why print them in the church bulletin and then read them to the people? Does this not discourage the reading? Why turn the worship service into a promotional rally? This is a real problem.

I have been the "associate in charge of announcements," more often the pastor saddled with making the announcements, and at other times one in the pew listening to announcements. I simply make a plea for brief, pointed and only necessary announcements, either before the worship begins or at the close. They should never take more than three minutes. The church is probably trying to promote too much if more time is necessary. To go beyond this is an exercise in futility. As I have discovered as one in the pew, people resent long announcement periods so much that they simply tune them out.

When the announcements are made at the close of the worship period, it can then be quite appropriate for the minister to say, "The worship is concluded. Let us now begin the service."

Preaching As Worship

Preaching the Word may be the main part of worship and should be an act of worship by the preacher. God, not the preacher, is the great end of preaching.

If the pastor is to be the change agent he feels himself to be, perhaps one of the better ways is to do what sometimes is called "confessional preaching." In this type of proclamation he shares his own struggles as he seeks to live out the Christian life. People are then more attracted to him to share their needs and their struggles, and together fellowship is built as the communication processes increase and barriers are broken down.

Writing in the *Baptist Program*, Dr. D. P. Brooks pleaded for integrity in the pulpit. Referring to Bible interpretation, he deplored allegorizing and spiritualizing. He said in part:

We have some allegories in the Bible, and they need to be interpreted as just that. But a parable is not an allegory. The parable makes one main point. To press other details into some allegorical pattern is dishonest....Any pastor who starts proof texting, spiritualizing, or allegorizing passages that were never intended to be taken thus needs to take a hard look at the bitter fruit of that form of interpretation in the past. It enabled a church to take the best, most intelligent, and most dedicated people of the time and murder them. They were strangled, drowned, burned at the stake, broken on the wheel, banished, and put in dungeons. What were their crimes? They interpreted the Bible according to the dictates of their consciences instead of rubber stamping the doctrines of a corrupt church.

Spiritualizing is another snare. The spiritualizing preacher reads a text and promptly departs from it. He may say some true and timely things to the congregation, but they are not rooted in the Bible passage he reads. If he did not mean to give an honest exegesis and interpretation of the text, why did he not find another text that does say what was needed?

A fairly large body of consensus exists among Bible scholars about the basic requirements for responsible interpretation. Here are a few that doubtless would find broad acceptance. While following them will not end all differences and solve all problems, it will greatly lessen the field of difference and give a basis for responsible dialogue.

1. Determine the exact meaning of the text. The first question we should ask is: What did the writer say? This involves going back to the original language in which the text was written. Scholarly sources enable any serious student to get the root meanings of the Hebrew or Greek

words in the text. Until this step has been taken the preacher has no right to pretend to interpret the scripture.

2. What literary form did the writer use? Did he write poetry or prose? Is it straightforward prose; or is it a parable, an analogy, a prayer, a sermon, a prophesy, or a vision? We pervert the scriptures when we take passages that obviously were not meant to be taken literally and interpret them as straightforward prose. Similarly, we cannot interpret literally what is clearly symbolical without losing integrity and credibility.

3. The context of the passage must be allowed to throw light on the text. Proof texting is unworthy of a minister of the gospel. Most passages have to be set in the context of the book and the particular part of the book in which they occur. All must be set in the context of the entire Bible.

4. The historical and cultural setting must be recognized. Who was speaking? To whom? And what did it mean as originally spoken or written? Many verses in the Bible are not presented as truth of God. Job's friends delivered speeches in which they made many false assertions. God condemned them and their views. Not only the word of God, but also the words of men appear in the Bible – some of men's words recorded are false and devilish. *Only one who wants to make the Bible say what he wants it to say would fail to take account of the meaning the passage had in the original setting.*

5. Every Christian interpreter must interpret the Bible in the light of Christ. He is God's supreme Word to us, the clearest revelation of the character and intent of our Creator. Therefore, any interpretation that is contrary to the spirit of Christ must be rejected. If the church had held to that principle during the Dark Ages, the ages would not have been so dark. "If any man have not the Spirit of Christ he is none of his" (Rom. 8:9).

6. The final question to be asked of a Bible passage is this: What does it mean now? Until we have determined the exact statement of the passage and the original meaning when spoken, we are not qualified to interpret the meaning of the passage.

Preachers who fail to deal honestly and reverently with the scriptures have a problem of credibility and of integrity.

A good statement from the Old Testament concerning the preaching ministry could well be: "Men who have an understanding of the times and who know what Israel ought to do." This means being alert to the challenges of the day as well as being aware of what God's Word has to say.

A New Testament criterion for preaching is, "There is a lad here." Keep him in mind as you preach. Can he understand you? Do you feed the lambs? It is unethical to overlook them in your congregation.

Do you represent Christianity or churchianity in your preaching? Are you building an institution or preaching Christ? One's preaching must not frustrate. A church member said, "I would like to do what the pastor wants, but what does he want?"

While one's preaching must inspire, it must have heart power as well as head power since one never moves the will until he appeals to the emotions. Inspirational preaching is different from emotional preaching. One preacher was said to have had in his notes: "Cry here." And later in his notes: "Cry here if you can."

So it is unethical to distort or exaggerate facts, and certainly it is an abuse of the scriptures to try to prove a point on the basis of facts that are distorted. Much of what is called exegesis in the modern day proof-texting type of preaching is more "Isogesis." If the pastor is to be ethical in his approach to Bible study, he will try to avoid "Isogesis" and find exactly what the scripture says instead of what "I" think or "I" believe. Further, it is unethical to preach all legalism and no grace. But on the other hand, it would be unreal to preach grace without the law. In one's preaching it is unethical to ignore injustice and corruption in the community with one's personal security in mind. However, one should be careful in his approach and shouldn't feel that he always *must* speak out openly about everything. But to avoid involvement or speaking out on church/community relations is unbecoming to a man of God, whether in the pulpit or out of it.

Ethical Evangelism

The invitation may be the climax of worship. The aspirations and resolves by members *should* crystallize in decisions. The decisions should be verbalized by the preacher to lead the congregation to respond. The response may not always be visible.

There are many pastors who in their preaching ministry and personal visitation are unethical in their evangelism approaches. They lessen the demands of the gospel in order to get more numerical results and manipulate people to make professions of faith or decisions. It is very easy to confuse movement of the people for movement of the Spirit or to judge results of revival by the actions of the people in the church house rather than by their actions at home and in their dealing with their fellowman. A church does not have an authentic spiritual revival until it affects the behavior patterns of the membership.

So, as Hoppin says: "True worship is the edifying of the people in all Christian faith and godliness; it does this by leading men to God in prayer, song, reading of the scripture and preaching; by developing the divine life, the real Christian feeling, the true spirit of Christian love that's in the people – warming into new growth and activity every power and quality of the Christian life."

Prepare Members for Worship

Many ministers criticize the members for their failure to worship, and to do so is unethical unless the pastor is attempting to prepare the members for worship by:

1. Training them to enter the place of worship promptly and quietly.

2. Encouraging personal prayer and preparation for the experience of worship.

3. Encouraging joyful participation and corporate worship experiences.

4. Teaching value of silence in worship – sensitivity and receptivity in the Spirit's leadership.

5. Training in the art of listening and participation in the worship.

6. Training in recognition of the moment that blends the congregation in corporate worship.

7. Training in the place of the invitation in worship.

8. Training in understanding the relationship between worship and fellowship.

Essence of Fellowship

Fellowship is more than a glad hand. Superficial contact is often passed for fellowship in the church, and people move on, lonely and anxious and craving fellowship and supportive friendships. One of the most difficult tasks is to develop the membership into a real koinonia. This is not done through content-centered, self-interest groups, but through leading the people to share themselves with others as whole persons. New Testament koinonia was an experience of profound sharing, of intense belonging, and intimate fellowship of Christians which was first experienced in small person-to-person groups.

The brotherhood of Christians is one of a spiritual creation. Human fellowship is based upon our common fellowship with Christ. So the members need to be trained in the fine art of living together. The chief weakness of our church is in our dwarfing affections and our stunted sympathies. We may be rich in money, building and equipment, members and ideas but poor in love. Those who are interested enough in the advancement of the

Kingdom to build the church as an institution but not sufficiently interested in people as persons will have a difficult time building a real Christian fellowship.

The source of warmth in the church is human fellowship. Because many churches are audiences rather than brotherhoods, we have much loss through the back door. An audience is a crowd, but a church is a family. An audience may be a gathering, but the church is a fellowship. Ministers are ordained not to attract audiences but to build churches. It is hard work, and the pastor needs the prayers and sympathetic understanding and help of the members, for no man can preach love effectively over the body of a loveless church. Perhaps, therefore it should be said that our task is not to Christianize the world but to Christianize the church and let the church be a witness to the world. The minister must utter the thought of God in such a way as to bind together the largest number of Christian hearts in the closest kind of fellowship for Christ-like service.

Building Fellowship among New Members

How can the pastor do this in an ethical way? A few practical suggestions:

1. The shepherd must always walk the path of love from the study to the pulpit. To some members, the pastor seems to lose his love when he steps into the pulpit.

2. We initiate the new member into this fellowship by helping him feel at home. This can be done by the manner in which he is received and how his experience is verbalized. We can follow up with opportunities for him to become acquainted with other church members as well as the church staff.

3. The new member can receive instruction concerning the mechanics of church operation and how he may participate:

a. By the use of orientation classes or similar group activities.

b. By careful induction into the advisable and available organizations.

c. By encouraging his participation in some social activities.

d. By not assuming too much, such as his knowing our names, or his spiritual growth, his motivation or his abilities.

e. By encouraging members to visit new members – not for the sake of anything "churchy" but pure interpersonal relationships.

4. We can lead the new member to help with homework. This involves utilizing training activities, perhaps an apprenticeship type of visitation effort, developing some group learning situations without a sales pitch or axe to grind but which will contribute to his spiritual growth. It is unethical to give spiritual birth to a baby and not provide a crib and a layette. Dr. Walley tells of inviting a man in California to attend church, and the man replied,

"Aren't Baptists the group who dips then and *drops them?*" Think about this in terms of *your* church's relationship to new members.

Ministering in Grief

At the other end of the family life circle, there are the older people. One young pastor posed this problem: "I have such a large number of older people that I'm constantly conducting funerals and then neglecting the relatives following the initial experience of sorrow. Do you have any suggestions?" My suggestions were:

1. Mark in your date book a time to visit the family one week past the funeral – and do it.

2. Mark in your date book a time to visit two weeks from that time, and then three weeks, and then a month. Depending upon the circumstances, you may have to go more often. Then a little later you may not need to visit quite so much. Scheduled planning of follow-up will enable you to keep from neglecting someone who has special need of your help.

The Untouchables

Someone has said that the army of the Lord is the only one in which they shoot the wounded. The statement is made in reference to the treatment by pastors and church family people of alcoholics, divorcees and other people who are a part of the church's "leper colony" – the untouchables. Dozens of time I've heard the lament from a divorced person: "I find that I do not have a Christian friend in my church, one who will come to me or one to whom I can go, who understands my needs. My pastor shuns me; my Sunday school teacher gives me little attention. At a time when I need someone so much, there seems to be no one to turn to." If these were isolated cases, it would be bad enough. But they are very common.

"Brethren, if a man be overtaken in a fault, ye which are spiritual restore such a one in the spirit of meekness, considering yourself lest ye also be tempted" (Gal. 6:1). Maybe the key here is *ye which are spiritual.* It is unforgivable to neglect those in the leper colony. Jesus touched them. Surely the pastor can make himself available.

What do you say to them? Why say anything? Except "I'm praying for you." "I'm sorry." "I care." "I'm concerned." "Is there anything I can do?" "I'm ready to listen – to cry with you – to pray with you." Read Romans 12:9-13. Pick up such words as "brotherly love," "affection and concern," "unselfish consideration," "earnestness," "spirit control," "patient," "prayerful," "compassionate," and "hospitable." Perhaps this says it best about how the minister should behave toward the members.

The Right Hand of Fellowship

What about the right hand of fellowship that is a practice in some churches? See Galatians 2:9. The right hand of fellowship was not the glad hand of welcome but the hand of agreement to divide the work in a missionary enterprise. They agreed on their tasks. They sealed their commitment with the right hand of fellowship. In our day, it is to say to those who come into our church family: "We rejoice in your fellow- ship in the work of Christ and in your commitment to him. We, too, have our work. You do your job; I'll do mine. Let's clasp hands on it."

In building up the body of Christ we must build persons up in loving fellowship with each other. In Luke's gospel we read of the two on the way to Emmaus who, as they walked with the Lord, later recalled their experience saying, "Did not our hearts burn within us as he walked with us and talked with us in the way?" Somehow the pastor must lead his people to compare hearts before comparing notes.

Checking with Ushers

If consideration and common courtesy are two hallmarks of a pastor's ethical behavior, it is appropriate for us to consider such minute details as checking out the public address microphone to ascertain the correct volume for comfort of the congregation as well as assisting the pastor to be heard. The same principle would apply to checking out the lighting system, heat and ventilation, and to arrange signals between the pastor and ushers to control these without public reference to them. Ushers should be trained to handle disturbances that may arise in the congregation, such as some emotionally disturbed person coming in from the outside, children who become obnoxious by making constant trips to the restroom or water fountain, and young people who may thoughtlessly distract others by their conversations during the service.

Disturbance in Worship

One pastor observed two young men in the balcony misbehaving during the worship service. Rather than embarrass the entire congregation, he asked one of the young men after the service the question: "How should a Christian young man behave in a church service?" The youth replied, "Reverently." "Thank you," said the pastor. "That's all I wanted to know." Writing about this fifteen years later in a denominational magazine, the young man, then a foreign missionary, reported: "That's one lesson I never forgot."

In event of public disturbance of a serious nature, a pastor simply has to follow what good common sense dictates at the time. He must remain calm in times of danger, as when the building is on fire. Giving assured directions to evacuate the building and seeing that all reach safety would be his primary concern. Again, the circumstances at the time will dictate the proper response.

Protecting from Hazards

The pastor has some ethical responsibility in insisting that fire and accident hazards be corrected. Certainly he should lead the congregation to carry out suggestions made by the fire marshal or others interested in safety of people in the community. There are some who seem to feel that because they are a church they are above the law in these respects.

The Simple Things

Do not overlook the simple acts of kindness people may feel the minister is above doing. Remember that "Jesus ate with sinners." This was a revolutionary idea! Do not fear to do the unusual. But I don't believe a minister should be fanatical or, on the other hand, drip with piousity. He should not be concerned about hanging spiritual scalps on his belt, but a well-placed, unexpected telephone call, an affirmation or an expression of appreciation and Christian love will do wonders in building Christian fellowship, especially if such is directed to one who is usually overlooked. The heart and work of every minister gleams with a borrowed light, the glory of our Lord Jesus Christ.

"Our preacher had surgery today — he was opened with prayer."

6.

THE MINISTER IN CARE-GIVING

Most ministers of a local church desire to be good pastors. To do this, he knows that he must visit with the people, get to know them and help them feel he is a part of their lives. It has frequently been said that a house-going pastor makes a church-going people, but it is extremely difficult to do pastoral visitation in our time. How do you find people at home? How do you keep from spending too much time seeking them?

System and Flexibility

Some ministers carry out a systematic plan of visitation by appointment, writing notes in advance which state when they plan to visit and requesting members to phone if the time is not convenient. This avoids considerable lost motion. Late afternoon, evening and Saturday are about the only times most people are home. This means that if the pastor gets around, he must make fairly brief calls. But surely one must avoid making calls just for the sake of the number of visits made or being able to say he has *stuck his foot in the door* of each home of his membership.

However a pastor visits, he must be careful not to convey the impression that he's in such a hurry that he really doesn't have the time to spare. Simplicity, sincerity and spiritual purpose should always be the marks of a pastoral call. He must be adaptable. He must be at ease whatever he faces, for when the pastor is uneasy, the members themselves become apologetic, nervous or embarrassed. If he drops in unexpectedly and finds circumstances embarrassing to the member or to himself, he must be careful not to preach, but visit. His very presence is enough to induce guilt without his adding an admonition from the Lord. This is not the time to impose his own eccentricities upon the family. For example, one minister found a young matron who was a prospect for the church smoking a cigarette. He told her that she was going to hell if she did not give up tobacco. After the visit, she did not consider herself a prospect for membership in his congregation.

Another *for instance*: A pastor, calling on an unaffiliated person, was invited to sit at the table with the man, who had a bottle before him. The man said, "Pastor, I won't be so rude as to invite you to have a drink with me for I know you don't drink, and I want you to know that the bottle here is not an affront to you, nor do I mean any disrespect. But about this time every afternoon I begin drinking and drink until bedtime."

The pastor replied, "I appreciate your explanation, and I would hope that you might see fit to give up your drinking because of the potential

57

danger to your health; but I did not come here to talk about that; I came to get acquainted with you."

This adaptation and the cultivative visitation that followed resulted in spiritual blessing to both the pastor and his host.

A pastor may need to adapt to filth and bad manners. He may need to ask if he may turn the television down a bit to be able to carry on a conversation. Without apology he may suggest that he doesn't get around to see the families as often as he would like and wonders if there is anything he can do for them especially. Are there spiritual needs that he may be unaware of? The conversation may lead to the suggestion of a return visit or an office visit by some member of the family. This is a good opportunity to get the names of the children fixed in his mind. His observation of the home may indicate something of the talents, achievements or special interests of family members. He may care to conclude the visit with a brief prayer or pastoral benediction. Sometimes conditions make praying inappropriate. He does not need to ask permission to pray as though he expects a negative response, but rather, "Shall we have a word of prayer together before I leave?"

In visiting during inclement weather he should remove his topcoat or outer garment and be seated as though he plans to stay a while. Even if the visit will be short, this conveys the valid impression that he has really come to visit and feels at home with them.

A good minister will go quickly to his people in trouble and will not hesitate to state the purpose of his visit. Again, this may not be a time for *preaching* but for "What can I do to help?" It could be that all he needs to do is *be there*. He doesn't have to try to explain things, philosophize or quote scripture; just being with them may be all that is needed.

Some pastors are able to do a great deal of family visiting at the church door on Sunday morning. One beloved brother, now deceased, would keep the people moving through the door at a very slow pace as he inquired about family members and what had been going on in the family. His church members loved this and were never in a hurry to leave and always wanted to go through the *pastor's door*. This was his special time with his people.

When a Member Is in Surgery

Is it possible that a minister can spend too much time with his people? Perhaps so. For example, he may be so conscientious about being with them during hospital experiences that he overlooks the needs of other members and finds himself working altogether as an emergency room technician. How can this be handled without neglect?

58

Example: Some pastors have the practice of going to the hospital when members are facing surgery and staying with the family all through the surgery period. With medical techniques of our time, this could last several hours. One pastor found an approach that he felt worked just as well in ministering to the spiritual needs of his people. He was always at the hospital early to pray with the patient before sedation or other last minute preparation. He stayed with the family while the patient was taken to the operating room and had prayer with them in the room. Then, unless there were unusual circumstances, he went to the church office, indicating that he would check back later and did so a couple of times during the period of the operation. The family was asked to call if they needed him. Thus following the progress of the operation, he tried to return before the doctor reported to the family and decided then how much longer he should stay, depending upon the circumstances. While this method involved some travel back and forth to the hospital, it also gave him opportunity to visit other members in the hospital, but taking care not to carry emotional germs from one hospital room to another. This pastor found that church members became aware of his sense of obligation to other members, or to prior commitments, but at the same time ministered to their special spiritual needs.

Visiting Where There Is Contagious Disease

Sometimes the pastor feels he must visit and risk the possibility of contracting a contagious disease. He should use his best judgment in protecting himself and other members of his own family and congregation. This could mean wearing a face mask, being very careful about washing his hands after visiting the sick (before he leaves the hospital) and other means that would help avoid contagion. He may find that a telephone inquiry would be just as appropriate as a visit and perhaps even more appreciated. If, however, there is an indication that his presence is needed, surely he must put aside his concern for his own safety and do his very best. It is neither ethical nor courageous to be foolhardy in such matters.

The Pastor as a Member of the Healing Team

Since we have a long tradition of pastors visiting the sick, we are treating this subject at length. Family members often are solicitous that the pastor is aware that illness exists, while others expect him to learn by radar or microwave. Many feel offended if they are hospitalized and the pastor does not show.

Illness or accident bids for the attention of the pastor to the family as well as to the patient and gives him an opportunity for a supportive, comforting, therapeutic role. Obviously, much good is done by per- forming this pastoral function. Yet, like the woman in the Bible who suffered much by many physicians, some patients and families suffer too much from many preachers.

Negative Patterns

What are some negative patterns of pastoral behavior? To mention a few:

• To dispense prayers like pills.

• To use the Bible as a prescriptive cure-all, piously quoting scripture as though that settles it.

• Undermining confidence in the medical doctor by suggesting that "perhaps Dr. X should be called in since he is more of a specialist in this field."

• By weakening the faith of the patient in sharing the *good news* that Bro. Doe almost died last week with what you have, but he pulled through and looks like he is going to make it now.

• By prescribing a *home remedy* or treatment other than that being suggested by the physician.

• By being effervescently optimistic with an approach that evades reality, avoids the seriousness of the patient's and family's need and makes the people wish he would *drop dead.*

• By carrying emotional germs from one patient to another, reporting especially on the incurables. "So you think you've got troubles. You ought to see the patient in 247."

• By carrying an unwelcome, gloomy attitude that creates depression and sadness and consequently impairs treatment.

• By imposing his delightful companionship for an hour upon a patient recovering from surgery and badly in need of rest.

• By talking rather then listening, thus not learning what the fears, anxieties or spiritual needs of the patient really are.

• By being judgmental in attitude. "Too bad you are not a good enough Christian to avoid this." "If one's faith is strong enough, he does not need tranquilizers." "I hope when you get out of here you will get back in church where you have belonged all the time" – thereby inferring that the illness is sin and guilt induced.

New Methods

There have been developments in medicine and psychiatry that should result in some changes in pastoral methodology. The medical profession has realized that they must be concerned for the person as a whole. Personality factors may speed or retard the healing process and in many instances determine whether the patient will live or die. The minister also must discover the biblical doctrine of the whole man.

The biblical mandate, "Heal the sick" (Matt. 10:8), and the fact that "Jesus went about healing all manner of sickness and disease" were long thought to be sufficient for the healing professions – the hospital ministry plus an adjunct to the command to "pray for the sick." The oft-used phrase by hospitals and nurses, "I dressed his wounds; God healed him," has been the gist of the healing concept. The Bible calls the body the "temple of the Holy Spirit" (I Cor. 6:19). The supreme witness of God's love is revealed in the incarnation of Jesus Christ, in his taking the likeness and fashion of a man with all the consequences that are involved, including suffering and death (Phil 2:6,7). The physiological harmony of the body, the working together of all its organs, is presented as the image that should reign in the church through love (I Cor. 12:12-30). The resurrection promised us is not just the immortality of the soul but rather a personal resurrection, a resurrection of the whole person with a body as well as a soul (Phil. 3:21).

In the Bible it is clear that what distinguishes man from the rest of nature is that he is made in the image of God and thus is capable of personal fellowship with God and of control over the rest of God's creation.

Implications of Illness

There are many and varied theological implications in illness itself. It is said that the average person has from ten to twelve illnesses per year, including colds and intestinal upsets. Some questions raised in the mind of a sick person are:

1. Why did I get sick?
2. Why did this happen to *me*?
3. Why did this happen *now*?
4. How will this illness affect my family?
5. How will it affect my job?
6. How long will I be sick?
7. How will I ever pay this hospital bill?
8. What will be the outcome? Will I be disabled? Die?

As people think about their illness in terms of theological implications, they may feel or express one or more of the following:

1. God does not know about me. It is just one of those things. God does not know or care about me.
2. God is testing me.
3. God let me down. I've lived a good life, so God has not kept His end

61

of the bargain.

4. God is mad at me. (Patient feels guilt and thinks God is punishing him.)

5. I don't believe in God anymore. (He is angry because God has allowed this illness.)

6. If God will heal me, I'll serve Him. (Barter for health concept.)

Now these are all faulty views of both God and illness. May we suggest the following as more appropriate Christian concepts:

1. God knows and cares about my illness.

2. God will help me through this (This is not necessarily faith in recovery but faith in God's love and presence regardless of the prognosis.)

3. I am partly responsible for this, maybe from worrying, eating, drinking, smoking or working too much.

4. I can learn something from this experience.

5. God has helped me to endure more than I ever thought I could.

6. I will always hope!

In the crisis of illness, there is a special kind of dependency, a definite kind of loneliness, certain limitations that involve some spiritual intangibles; it is a time for reevaluation of values and the possible reordering of one's life. So an illness often takes on the dimensions of a religious experience.

Instant Healing – Divine Healing

Jesus said to the man with 38 years of affliction: "Do you *want* to be healed?" Some don't want to give up their dependencies.

Jesus commanded the man with the withered hand: "Stretch out your hand." We must do what *we can* to regain health.

Jesus told the woman with the hemorrhage: "Your faith has made you well." Faith does play a large part in recovery.

And Jesus suggested that we ought to thank God for His part in the cure. "Were not ten cleansed?" He asked the lone leper. "Where are the nine?"

In religious circles in recent years, there has been an upsurge of *divine healing* groups, reaching into old and respectable denominations where ministers and workers formerly scoffed at such as being fakery and religious racketeering, exploiting those who were victims of psychosomatic illnesses and such. For the person of faith, one cannot question the power of God to impose supernatural law over natural law. One can still pray for a miracle. Any honest doctor, even though an atheist or agnostic, sees patients improve and recover from conditions where the one plausible prognosis was deterioration and death.

To the person of faith, all healing is divine in the sense that nature provides recovery, retraining, rebuilding, recuperation and healing in accord with the principles established by the Creator with His creatures. So there are those who have come to believe in *instant healing* that is divine as well as *gradual healing* that is voluminous. On the other hand, many medical men will testify that during the time "healing services" are being held by many of the healing revivalists, members of the revival teams have sought treatment from the medical profession. Though I know of some "miracle" healings and do not discredit them, I am disposed to believe that God still wants both pastor and physician on His healing team in a cooperative, therapeutic ministry. Dr. Walley states, "I always pray for my patients, but I cannot think of a time where God intervened until I had done all I knew to do."

The Healing Touch

I am also convinced that both physical and spiritual healing may be aided by the *appropriate* human touch. Jesus once asked as He perceived that power had gone from Him, "Who touched me?" Often we read of His *touching* the eyes, the ear, the limb – and wholeness was the result. The early church fathers laid their hands on the sick and prayed for them. There may be therapeutic value in the appropriate human touch. Note my word *appropriate*. In certain situations one should not be near enough a patient to touch him. Shaking hands is out of order and so is shaking the bed, especially when one is taking a drip.

It is never appropriate to carelessly touch a sick person. One must remember that sick people are often supersensitive, so be very careful about gestures that could be misunderstood. Nevertheless, to help establish a feeling of empathy and identification, the light touch of the hand can be a valuable aid. When the patient extends a hand as you may suggest prayer, it should be lightly grasped. Sometimes it is appropriate to lightly lay your hand on the lower arm or the hand of the sick one, or in the case of a child, a light touch on the brow.

These are among the appropriate ways. Not always do we pray with the patient. The lingering touch of concern may be the gesture with a parting word. Under certain circumstances a pat on the shoulder by a physician may be most reassuring. So, with common sense, Christian compassion and discretion being the guide, do not overlook the healing ministry of the human touch.

Pastor-Physician Relationships

The common meeting ground between pastor and physician is in the area of the patient's emotions. Here are a few simple observations concerning these relationships:

1. The doctor-minister is forced into a joint relationship. It may not be a cooperative relationship.

2. The physician-pastor relationship is colored by the personal experience and background of each.

3. Either may take the initiative in establishing cooperative relationships, but in my judgment, the initiative usually lies more with the pastor than the doctor.

It is not always possible, especially in an urban setting, but is very helpful for the doctor and minister to know each other as persons rather than only in a professional setting. This should help develop assurance that each understands his role in reference to the other and in this cooperative relationship of the healing team. This does not exclude the doctor from praying for his patient and doing what he can for the alleviation of emotional difficulties and excessive tension that may affect the healing process.

4. Most doctors will recognize the minister's place. The minister must learn what his place is. The crucible of experience becomes our best teacher. When the cooperative team approach is employed, it may aid in the healing of the patient, help to the doctor and bless the minister.

5. The physician determines the diagnosis and determines the therapeutic approach. The pastor is guided by the physician's findings and attempts to use his role in dealing with the emotional and spiritual processes. The pastor does not volunteer medical advice and as far as possible refrains from discussing the nature of the patient's illness (except in necessary listening). He avoids medical terminology. He helps increase the patient's confidence in the doctor. He should leave the room when the doctor comes in, but he should not hesitate to learn from the doctor (when urgency, emergency or crisis situations exist) what the doctor feels the pastor can do best in a supporting role.

6. In working with psychiatrists, the patient may be seeing both the minister and the doctor at the same time. Team work is vital when the patient feels that his condition is a reflection on Christian faith.

Sometimes the pastor may need to write referral notes or talk with the psychiatrist if he has had considerable previous experience with the patient. He is not to give his theory or diagnosis, but *facts*, such as (1) onset of difficulty, (2) family, (3) school, social, marital, work or religious adjustment.

The minister should recognize that he is unprepared to help the following groups: (1) a person who is psychotic, (2) a person who has a very serious personality disorder, (3) a psychopathic personality, (4) a person who may be a suicide risk regardless of the underlying condition.

7. There must be cooperation between pastor and doctor when the patient returns to the community. This is more necessary with a patient from psychiatry primarily because of the taboos that unfortunately still exist in some families and the general public.

8. One is constrained to mention one specific role the pastor may exercise: encouraging families about autopsy when the physician feels such is desirable.

9. Both doctor and minister should recognize the place of administrative policies in institutions of healing.

10. The pastor should be alert to his obligation at times to render a "pastoral ministry" to the doctor.

11. When the minister is the doctor's patient, he should practice what the doctor preaches.

12. Both doctors and ministers should work together in preventive hygienic concerns for the elimination of disease.

This I believe: God has given to both the physician and the pastor the privilege of serving on this healing team. We are dealing with distressed and troubled people. We should not be over-assertive or over-anxious. We must be relaxed and confident without having a Messiah complex. We should have the courage to attempt our role even when we feel very inadequate, for "God is our refuge and strength, a very present help in time of trouble; therefore, we will not fear." And whether healing is "instant" or "gradual,"

> The healing of His seamless dress
> Is by our bed of pain,
> We touch Him in life's strain and stress
> And we are whole again.

7.
THE MINISTER AND OTHER STAFF MEMBERS

The senior minister should assume that the professional staff people are called, too. The "flaming bush" experience should be a part of the staff worker's experience. The demands are too exacting to shoulder unless they are God-called. There should be no seeking of place or position. The love of money must be burned out of one's life. There are family sacrifices to be made. There are prerequisites such as determination, perseverance, patience, gentleness, forgiveness, tact and love. The staff workers do not guide organizations but people who compose them. The burning bush experience leads one constantly along the path of the burning heart. This is the way of enlightened interpretation of the will of God and the place of Christ's disciple fulfilling that purpose in his time. Staff workers, whether male or female, cannot confine themselves to office hours. They must keep up with trends. They must exercise diligence to show themselves approved workmen (or women).

The price of success is keeping at it, always at it, everlastingly at it. In one's relation to God, he is not to be a fanatic but he may become so busy in the Lord's work that he may neglect the Lord himself. The pastor should recognize all of these factors with reference to the staff members. Herein lie some hazards: The hazard of despotism, seeking to run the show; the hazard of commercialism, seeking all sorts of favors and fringe benefits for himself and not enough concern for staff members in terms of financial remuneration for their services; the hazard of professionalism, feeling that the pastoral ministry is the most important gift. Surely those who feel called to the pastorate have recognized the significance of such a call, but all of the gifts are equal in importance as they are gifts of the Spirit. They may not be equal in responsibility or in privilege or in pay, but the professional calling, expertise, experience, training and position of the other staff members should be respected and affirmed by the pastor.

The staff worker should remember that the senior minister is the under-shepherd and by virtue of his position the spiritual leader of the church. Very few pastors disregard his high and holy calling to instead become a politician gifted in political maneuvering, or a business executive giving attention to detailed material things, thus leaving "the ministry of the word and prayer." So the staff worker should safely trust the pastor, receiving inspiration from working with him as well as from hearing him preach. The staff worker owes allegiance and loyalty to the pastor and when unable to give him *just dues* should resign. The worker should seek to make the pastor's dreams and ideals, when scriptural and worthy, come true. He should never try to fill his place. He has one of his own to fill. The more one helps the people love the pastor, the more they will love *him* and respond to his leadership. But the staff member should avoid building people around himself. It should be said of him, as of John the Baptist: "And the two disciples heard John speak and followed Jesus."

Pastors have different desires for their staff workers. I've heard these expressions: "I want him to work with me and not for me." "When I am away, I want to feel that the work is in good hands." "He understands the pastor's problems more than anyone else in the church, and I want him to help me with these problems." "I do not want him to be afraid of me. If he makes a mistake, I will stick by him; and if I make a mistake, he will stick by me." "I want her to watch details but not burden my ministry with them." "I want him to have initiative and vision and not be afraid to try them." "I don't want her to major on minor things." "I do not want him to turn into an odd-job man, yet I want him to feel like I do, that if a job needs to be done, do it." "I want him to love me and to fall completely in love with the people of the church. His love of folks must be right next to his love for the Lord."

Other workers should have the same interest and be just as willing to step in the gap as the pastor does. They should not expect any more definition of duties then does the pastor. They should be true yoke-fellows in every sense of the word.

There should be clear-cut job descriptions for each staff member of the church. It should spell out such things as days off and vacation time as well as responsibilities of the task.

There are difficulties and hindrances. Pastors often do not know how to divide responsibility. As before observed, they face the hazard of their vocation – the hazard of despotism. Sometimes men who are in the ministry are puffed with pride in their own conceits. They mistake practice for experience. Many pastors with long tenures of office boast of their long experience, when in reality they have only had a long practice. One does not have experience until he intelligently studies the results of practice and applies the lessons learned to improve future practice.

Some insist on their methods no matter how archaic because they fear the unfamiliar and new. Their pretense of superiority rises out of their own feelings of inferiority, and they thus resist change. The usual tendency of one following such a pattern is that of disregarding the will of the church, riding rough-shod over opposition, pushing aside those who differ, and catering to those who can be used as puppets to further the political ends of the pastor who becomes power conscious.

Many church members shift responsibility to the pastor because of their own laziness or desires, and they cater to the possible temptation to use his power wrongly. This situation may exist subconsciously, not to be revealed until another staff member is added and the problem of dual leadership and division of responsibility is presented.

Pastors are sometimes unwilling to share honors. Here they face the hazard of professionalism. Old green eyes, jealousy, marks the beginning of the end or hinders otherwise pleasant pastor/staff member relationships. Occasionally, jealousy exists in the heart of a staff worker, but sometimes it eats like a cancer in the pastor's soul. Hitherto, he has had all the favors, all the praises, and worn all the flowers. If the staff member does his job as the pastor and the church desire, there are compliments passed, friendships formed, evaluations made. Sad, but true, there are some little men in the ministry who simply can't take it! They cannot discern that those with genuine love and appreciation always have plenty to go around while flattery caters to nothing but itching ears. Love is never jealous. Envy or selfish ill-will toward another because he possesses what we desire for ourselves is a mark of the infantile. Jealousy in the extreme may reach the point of hatred, yet Christian workers sometimes allow it to fester in their hearts.

Should the pastor feel that the other worker is infringing upon his prerogatives, he should prayerfully counsel with him. One must not excuse himself for unholy tendencies on the ground that *after all, I'm human,* for all Christian workers, more especially the undershepherd and bishop of souls, should be more than human, demonstrating the fruits of the Spirit. If all cultivate the proper spirit, they may know the glory of a fruitful ministry, the chief mark of which is humility. Pastor and staff members may well share the tributes paid by those who are appreciative and rejoice that they are counted worthy to be laborers together with God.

The senior minister may take the initiative of publicly commending the staff worker in his or her leadership in a particular way such as a worthy project begun or completed. He may lead the congregation in observance of anniversaries, birthdays or other special days. He may express confidence by asking him to substitute in some usual pastoral prerogative. Caution must be observed to avoid imposition, and the appreciation expression must not be viewed as "damning with faint praise."

Pastors may be unwilling to share denominational and cultural privileges and in so doing become prey to the hazard of commercial-ism. They are warned by Paul not to love money. There will always be, and should be, some difference in the pastor's salary and that of other staff members. This has adjusted itself in some churches, and wide gaps should be narrowed as quickly as possible. The staff worker frequently has as many demands on him as the pastor in the way of personal appearance, necessity of automobile, comfortable living quarters, family expense, educational expense, entertainment and support of local and denominational programs. The pastor should use his influence to remedy any unfairness. Contrary to the opinion of many pastors, fairness on the part of the pastor will pay dividends in the attitude of the members toward the pastor's support. This consideration should include amounts for conventions, assemblies, retreats, and seminars. The pastor who takes the initiative to see that adequate provision is made for the staff member in these areas will not lack for consideration in his own behalf by the deacons and/or finance committee. Most church members want to be fair and do right, and sometimes their attention needs to be called to existing circumstances. The pastor *can* do it and *ought* to do it, but if he wants to always court the favor of the "denominational big-wigs" (favorite term of some pastors), or if he enjoys too much the privileges of travel on comfortable expense accounts or in any way has stumbled over the hazard of commercialism, in all probability he will *not* do it.

Lack of Mutual Planning and Promotion

Before any major programs are launched, there should be mutual planning on the basis of mutual goals. Too many plans fail due to the lack of adequate understanding. Whatever plans are determined then should be mutually promoted. The place of the pulpit is to inspire and provide incentive while the educational program should provide the techniques for achieving what the pulpit has declared to be scriptural and right. If a program is not worthy of pulpit mention in preaching and otherwise, it is not worthy of being attempted by the church. The staff members who do not have the *inspirational* assistance of the pastor will be lacking in *perspirational* assistance from the pew.

Areas of Special Emphasis

1. *Should the staff worker visit?* Visit the sick? Not when the pastor is on the field unless asked to do so by him. Some pastors believe in a shared ministry with the staff. Certainly, he should visit friends within the church family just as he would visit any other ill friend.

Upon the unchurched? Yes, he should set an example of evangelism both for the sake of the people and for his own spiritual growth.

Potential leadership? By all means. The importance of the work demands personal contact in enlistment.

New members? If asked to do so. The staff worker will become better acquainted with new members if he visits, and the pastor does not. But somebody must! And the new members should be visited to discover new talent for leadership. The plan of visitation should be agreed upon by the pastor, staff workers and the church. Proper publicity should be given the plan so that all the church members are informed.

2. *Should the staff member be a personal counselor?* The pastor is the divinely accredited representative, having a privileged relationship with people in intimacy from cradle to the grave; therefore, the pastor should be considered the chief-counselor of the church, but the staff worker will find himself being consulted on special problems. There are wide varieties of human need with which he must deal. There are problems of money, health, recreation, spiritual growth, and decision making. The need is for real love with as much psychological skill as possible. If the worker has not had special training, he should refer people to those who can handle difficult cases. Certain problems should be referred immediately to the pastor.

Some examples: Those that necessitate pastoral decisions; those where the pastor would have special expertise by virtue of his knowledge of family background or his ability to handle the problem; and those where only the pastor can tap resources adequate for the task.

In some matters, however, the fact the individual turns to the staff worker reflects the confidence in and imposes an obligation upon that worker which cannot be dismissed lightly.

Perhaps it is wishful thinking but assuming some staff members read this section, let me make a few more observations about counseling.

One must avoid the wrong methods. Among the popular methods in disrepute are: (1) being afflicted with dogmatics, (2) exhortation – delivering your soul, (3) use of suggestions, (4) the catharsis experience where the individual is led to unburden himself and goes out empty, and (5) intellectualized interpretation where the worker attempts to change the attitude by explanation or the treatment being a sort of diagnosis in reverse, the counselor thinking that if a person understands *how he got that way*, immediately his problem is solved. It does frequently help. However, these approaches are wrong as they assume that the staff member decides the goals and values for the individual. No one has the moral right to assume such choices for another person. The suggestion to *pray about your problem* sometimes aggravates the situation, as most people do not know how to do such praying and the suggestion only keeps the problem in the focus of attention. The writer suggests a good survey reading course in the field of pastoral counseling, with the caution that one should not consider himself a specialist after a six-week survey. Applied common sense combined with a good dose of religion saturated with genuine concern coupled to a listening ear and an understanding heart are your best assets. Practice loving listening and tread lightly on expert advice.

3. *What of marriages and funerals?* Only if the staff worker is ordained does this pose a problem. These are pastoral prerogatives. The pastor may solve the problem by asking the worker to assist and having it understood that he is to be called on when the pastor is away. When calls come from outside the church family, these may well be shared. An ordained associate works to an advantage as such demands need not interfere with vacation, revival schedules, or convention trips. Here the pastor holds the key to cooperation. He can be jealous of his rights or he may elect to share privileges to the joy of the church membership and the mutual larger influence of the two workers. When approaches for such service are made directly to the associate from outside the church membership, he has no choice but to perform the services to the best of his ability. When made from within, he must be governed by his understanding with the pastor and the circumstances at the time. It seems that in the tender and intimate experiences of the marriage ceremony or in grief, the family should have the privilege of choice; however, in the ethics of a profession (sometimes thought of more highly than the feelings of the members) an understanding between associate and pastor is wise.

4. *What about criticism of the pastor?* Because the staff worker sometimes lives closer to the people than does the pastor, he may hear criticism. He should never invite it, engender it or pass it on to anyone except the pastor. Most of the criticism is too small to remember. One must hear it and then answer by defending the pastor or, if unable to defend, suggest that the person take the criticism directly to the pastor. If it is serious enough to be reported, one must report the source as well as the criticism. It is unfair to do otherwise. One must not become a gossip-carrier, and the staff worker must have the good judgment to discern between the serious and the trivial. The wise worker will protect the pastor from the trivial.

Staff Reports

Staff members should be permitted to report to the church and/or deacons or any other group to whom they feel a sense of accountability. There should be liberty to make recommendation in writing to any other group. Staff members are servants of the church. They should be called by the church, report to the church and when ready, resign to the church. There are those who delegate this responsibility to the pastor. I feel that this is contrary

72

to the nature of church organization as described in the New Testament. However, if the church desires to make such a delegation, this is also their privilege. The staff member should exercise his privilege to suggest new ventures for the church if progress is to be made. He should not hesitate to suggest proven procedures according to the denominational patterns. He ought to be careful about bringing in something foreign to the denominational program (no one denomination has a corner on all the good ideas); however, he should use initiative and ingenuity in adapting programs to the local situation. These programs should be discussed with the pastor before they are initiated.

What to Do When Staff Relations Break Down

It ought to be considered a mark of personal failure for our interpersonal relationships to break down with Christian people, whether with staff or others. Some pastors and other staff members are immature, spoiled, self-centered and neurotic in some way. All of us need to grow toward Christlikeness. We should not be proud of our immaturity. One can dwindle and become more dwarfed in soul or he can have a thrust of growth in a crisis experience in which he may find himself.

So what should one do? First, recognize the breakdown! Don't hide your head in the sand. Then you have some alternatives:

1. One staff member resigns.
2. All staff members resign.
3. Take it to the church. Get a *vote of confidence* – split the church.
4. Arouse the people. Get sympathy for the "underdog."
5. Seek to reestablish communication. Talk it out. Pray it through. Be Christlike and really forgive instead of talk or sing about it.
6. Seek professional counsel – including possible psychiatric care.

At any rate, here are some pointers to observe:

1. Try to understand the reason for the breakdown:
One feels another is not carrying his share of the load.
One has work habits that irritate another.
One does not recognize protocol.
One is not sensitive to the needs of another.
One interferes with the work of another.
One persists in a course of conduct already known to be obnoxious to another.
One may work off his hostility toward another as a "scapegoat."
There may be a change in health pattern of staff member or his family.

2. Seek to understand and admit your failure in the breakdown.

3. Seek objective counsel from some fair person whom you can trust.

4. Seek to face the breakdown with others involved. Do not try to persuade another to your point of view but strive to get the right answer.

5. Practice the New Testament principle of reconciliation.

6. Avoid, if possible, getting the church leadership and membership involved. (Staff members and the pastor usually must assume responsibility when churches split.)

7. If church leadership must be involved, staff members should surely indicate their desire that the situation be worked out without the church becoming split. The church fellowship is more important than the tenure of the pastor or other staff members.

8. Pray much.

9. Let time work. If there is an emotional blowup, see if you can let it subside somewhat before tackling the problem.

10. Walk in the other's shoes with integrity – no deception, no lies.

11. Reevaluate job descriptions versus expected functions in practice and see what adjustments can or should be made.

12. Do not damn each other with faint praise.

13. Seek to understand each other as persons. Have fellowship as persons. It is easier to get along as professionals with those you know as persons.

One of the most painful experiences a few pastors have to deal with is serious malpractice on the part of one of the staff members. If there is a personnel committee, protocol should be observed. The question is: Who is supposed to act? Another question: What effort should the pastor make to redeem the situation before church or committee action is taken? Whatever is done should be done in honesty and with directness. Such matters as not giving salary increases or withholding salary are certainly unethical. If it is necessary to terminate a staff member, some provision should be made for the person to save his dignity, giving him time to move or help him move, and encouraging the church family to be patient. In doing so, the ministry of the individual may be saved.

Church leaders, the congregation, the pastor – all should share in the responsibility for wrongdoing. Maybe the job description was not sufficient. Possibly there was not enough sensitivity to depression or other emotions. Perhaps gossip developed because too much of the staff member's time had been taken with certain individuals.

If a staff member has expressed regret and the desire to do better, surely the pastor will not attempt to cause trouble for him in his next place of service. The pastor should assume that the staff member rightly deserves a second chance. If a grave moral problem has persisted, then perhaps truth should be told if asked for. Responsible, ethical behavior would say so; but be sure of your facts.

One minister was about to be called to a church when an employee of a denominational institution gave an erroneous report concerning the minister's marital situation. He reported hearsay as fact. The committee was given the facts later, but damage was already done and the prospective pastor had to ask that his name not be considered. This is not to suggest that the will of God was thwarted, but it is to say that the institutional employee behaved quite unethically.

Immoral Conduct

In event of immoral conduct (that is, sexual misconduct, wife beating, child abuse, perversion of youth, misappropriation of funds) every attempt should be made to deal redemptively with the staff member. It could well be that he will have to resign his work, depending upon both the nature of the offense and the congregation's spirit of loving reconciliation.

Two of the most memorable hours of my life were spent in worship while passing through a Texas city where the congregation was facing up to a redemptive experience with a staff member. There was little discussion as they were all familiar with the facts, but much repenting, rededication, praying and finally a motion that the congregation forgive the offending brother. It seemed like the entire congregation of more than one thousand seconded the motion. And in a flood tide of grace, heaven came down. For almost an hour the members filed by to express love and caring! What a day! Imagine leaving church at 2 p.m. and not being hungry! As a stranger in their midst, I was caught up in the indescribable thrill of feeling, "Behold, how these Christians love one another."

But there are still those in the army of the Lord who shoot the wounded, so it doesn't turn out this way very often. Whatever needs to be done for the fellowship and reputation of the church may be done. But at least as far as the pastor is concerned, he can act with love and seek to meditate God's marvelous grace to the offender or offenders. "Let he who is without sin cast the first stone."

8.
THE MINISTER AND
THE COMMUNITY OF FAITH

Behavior toward Older Ministers

One of the most pathetic sights is to observe how some young ministers treat older preachers. They are often snubbed or ignored, sometimes rudely. Sometimes younger ministers do not know the price the older minister paid through training as well as experience to gain the wisdom he actually possesses. Wisdom does not come from books. On the other hand, some people do not learn from their experience and never gain wisdom.

In our day we rarely see the type of older minister who has a great deal of insecurity and compensates by ultra-authoritarianism that has a tendency to turn off the younger minister. Sixty years ago I found older men willingly shared their experience with the younger ones in most helpful ways. I also found them still hungry for fellowship and for feeding upon the Word. As a young pastor with three older ministers in my congregation, I sometimes felt insecure in their presence. Finally one of them said, "Pastor, I hope you understand we preachers in your congregation are your best supporters. We know what you are going through as you lead and as you preach. We are also redeemed sinners and need to be fed from the Word of God. So do your best in preparation and in preaching and know that we are praying for you and are being helped by you."

I have found that older ministers more often appreciate and encourage younger ministers and seek to cultivate their friendship. Granted, there are a few who see them as a threat as they feel they are being displaced by younger men in pastorates. On the other hand, as I deal with younger men in the ministry today, I have a hopeful feeling about the Kingdom. I believe the future is in good hands! For quite a while I have taken a fatherly stance toward younger men in the ministry and have often been free in my counsel to them. I've discovered that this counsel is much more acceptable when it is sought after than when I dispense it without being asked. This has been a struggle for me because I feel, as my esteemed professor, Dr. H. E. Dana used to say, "I do love to teach preachers; they have such large chunks of ignorance." The emphasis is both loving them and teaching them rather than just enjoying to talk about your own experiences.

Retired Former Pastors

A word should be said about the relationship of the minister with retired pastors and their wives who might live on the field. Immediately such phrases come to mind as "respect them," "love them," "visit with them," "fellowship with them," and "use them."

It is a very sad commentary on the attitude of some ministers when some of our more prominent pastors neglect the former pastor. For example: One man served a pastorate for thirty years and retired. He was much loved by the people. The new pastor visited him only once over a period of two years; and when the former pastor suffered a heart attack, he visited with him three times over a period of three months.

The retired pastor may be particularly helpful to his successor when people are sick or in trouble. He often has some insight into the family needs that the new pastor does not have. If his counsel is asked for, he would probably be glad to share.

One should not try to wean the people away from the retired pastor. If they have much love for him, be assured that they have enough to go around, and their hearts can be stretched to love you, too. Just thank God that he taught them to love their pastor or enabled them by being loving to thus love you, their present pastor. An unloving attitude by the new pastor toward the retired pastor can hinder the congregation from loving the new one.

Behavior toward the Widow of a Former Pastor

Occasionally the minister will find himself pastor of a former pastor's widow. These women are usually much loved by the church family. One pastor said of a former pastor's wife who was a member of his congregation: "I just hope I have the grace and the wisdom to conduct myself as well as this precious saint does." The pastor should be expected to give as much attention to this widow as he would any other widow in the congregation – perhaps a little more since there are opportunities for special recognition, as a church anniversary or some other special event. He can, without overdoing it, keep before the congregation the relationship that this lady has had to the life of the church.

Sometimes, the widow is in physical or financial need, and the pastor can lead the church family to respond to this need as they may be reluctant to do so without having his approval.

I knew one widow who was treated as a *nothing* – a non-entity. She was completely ignored by the pastor and his wife. I have also known similar situations in denominational circles. This also is a commentary on the insecurity of the current leader. I have known pastors to manipulate the widow of a former pastor to a very minor position in the life of the church, seemingly to circumvent some influence that he obviously felt she had.

But I've known many, many pastors who were kind, considerate and attentive. Such always cheers the hearts of relatives and friends in the church, and I believe this makes glad the heart of God. My eighty-six-year-old mother-in-law taught a Sunday school class until she was eighty-five. She had been a part of the life of her church for a forty-six years and a widow for thirteen years. Friends in the congregation greeted her constantly with loving affection including Christian embrace. One such friend was greeting her at the time the young pastor came by. The lady said, "The reason I love her so much is that she was my Sunday school teacher at the time my children were growing up and she taught me a whole lot." The pastor added an additional affirmation by saying, "I'm sure she could teach all of us a lot." Such pastoral appreciation and affirmation added to the joy of this widow of a former pastor.

Relationship with Former Pastors

Again words like "love," "respect their contribution and their methods" (as long as they were honorable) come to mind. You can introduce your own way of doing things without suggesting that past methods were *wrong*. In a growing congregation, one method works better at one time while another method is better at another time. It might be well to suggest to the congregation that when you change a method and it is not better than the one being used, they can always go back to what they had.

Encourage your people to love and appreciate the former pastor. Invite him back for some occasions. Let him know that he is always welcome at any time. Though there may be those in the congregation who do not appreciate him and may be slightly critical of your inviting him, most of this group could not care less. However, those who love him will also love you the more.

Sometimes you will need patience. One former pastor would read in the church bulletin that John Doe made a profession of faith or that Mrs. John Smith joined by letter and would send photostatic copies of his pastoral visitation record while pastor, indicating how many times he visited that family. It could be that he was saying, "One plants, another waters, and God give the increase." Or it could have meant, "Be careful, Brother, about taking the credit. I worked on that person, too. Share the glory with me." I prefer to think that he was accepting the former premise. If this should happen in your church, a note thanking the former pastor for his interest and prayers and joy in the decisions that were made would be in order.

In a situation where God did a monumental work while I served as pastor of the flock for a period of eight years, my successor and I have experienced a tremendous fellowship and friendship. Over a period of fourteen years we have corresponded and talked on the telephone occasionally, and I have been back for two homecomings and three revival emphases. When I am in the community, he mentions certain persons he thinks I should visit if I have time, who have special needs that he feels I can meet. On my visits, I sincerely commend the present pastor, and I think I am helping the people to love all the more.

If I have had particularly close ties to a family in grief, this pastor will ask, "Would you like for me to contact Dr. Hensley to see if he can come back?" Then he calls me if their answer is in the affirmative. I ask if there is some special reason why I *should* come, and if there is none, I, in turn, ask him to express my sympathy. Consequently, we have met this particular problem without any conflict or competing for attention or affection.

On several occasions travel has taken me through the city. I have called him, and we met a few miles outside of town for conversation about our personal interests, the work and people whom we both love.

Relationship with Pastors of Other Denominations

Again, words like respect, appreciate, commend, confer, and cooperate come to mind. One does not easily forget the kind of relationship established when the Baptist pastor moved to a new community and received a call from the Methodist pastor who was much loved. (It is proper for the resident pastor to make the first call or visit.) After a period of getting acquainted, the Methodist minister asked permission to pray and prayed earnestly for a fruitful work by the Baptist brother. You are not surprised that an unusual friendship developed.

After some years the Methodist minister suffered a heart attack but recovered from it. Later his church was in a revival meeting, and he asked his Baptist friend to preside for him one night, as he had inadvertently scheduled a wedding in another community. The instructions were to tell the congregation where he was as they might think "the old boy has had another heart attack." The next morning at 5 o'clock he *did* have a fatal heart attack. One would know that this Baptist pastor was among those most helpful to the grieving Methodist congregation.

You have many mutual problems and opportunities with other churches in various communities. Some ministers too often have been guilty of "hoeing in their own backyard" to such an extent that they could not join with the other brothers for a united front in dealing with community social problems. It casts a reflection upon all the denomination when one attends a ministerial alliance meeting in his community and informs the brothers that he does not like preachers, that he does not plan to be in any other ministerial meetings and that he just came to this one to let them know how he stands. If such should come from some inexperienced brother, we would not be too surprised; but for a man who has had significant responsibilities in a denomination to make such a pronouncement casts a shadow upon all.

Fellow Pastors

Literally dozens of times through the years I have heard some of the men out in the county refer to the county-seat pastor and say, "He really takes an interest in us and our needs and in our people." Or I have heard, "He never attends any of the associational meetings and hardly speaks to us when we meet him on the street. He takes no interest in our work and seems to think he is too good to associate with us." Or they rejoice when the county-seat pastor takes a vigorous, positive stand on some social issue and works with them for the moral improvement of the community and county.

Getting a little closer to home, surely most would agree, as stated before, that there should be no *sheep-stealing*. One pastor should not criticize another to his own members or to the pastor's members. In visiting mutual prospects, a good practice is to commend some positive features of the neighboring church and pastor while emphasizing the strengths of your own church fellowship and program.

Do not visit the other pastor's people unless requested to do so. Notify your neighboring pastor of his sick members if you learn about them and feel he does not know. If there is some relationship where you have a sense of obligation to visit someone in the hospital because he is your personal friend or a relative of one of your members who has requested you to make a call, then try to wait until your fellow pastor has the chance to go first.

Do not encourage disgruntles to join your church. They will probably become disgruntled there, too.

Share one another's burdens. Pray for each other. Be vulnerable enough to love each other unconditionally.

Minority Group Pastors

I feel that the pastor should take the initiative in getting acquainted on a friendship basis with any minority group pastor in his community. This relationship should be as one person to another and not as the strong meeting the weak. When a relationship is established on this basis, it is easy and natural for other things to follow which can be mutually beneficial.

In some areas, it is possible for the pastor to suggest a pulpit exchange and perhaps choir exchange occasionally. Dialog, appreciation, counsel, combined ministers' meetings are acceptable patterns in most communities. The pastor may teach seminary extension courses attended by minority group pastors or offer leadership training in his church to which minority groups are invited.

In the early fifties in a southern city where I was pastor, we followed the pattern of an integrated ministerial association, Good Friday and Easter observances, and Vacation Bible School activities.

These suggestions are based on the assumption that, though the church has an *open membership policy*, the community pattern essentially will be that of ethnic and minority congregations desiring to maintain identity as a church.

Denominational Relationships

It does not hurt the reputation of any pastor to be known as a strong denominational man. If he does not believe in the program of his denomination, he should be honest enough to get into one where he can work rather than disrupt the program to which he is only nominally committed.

When one pastor was approached by a member of his church with a question about a certain procedure, saying, "I do not think that is in accordance with the usual Baptist practice," the pastor replied, "We are not operating this church by Baptist principles and doctrine. We're running it to suit ourselves." Such an attitude should not exist in the heart of any pastor toward his denomination. This is not to suggest that he should rubber stamp or approve all that is recommended by denominational workers or that he should not use his influence for the principles and methods he believes to be right. But I contend that after trusted brethren in a democratic spirit have arrived at conclusions as to proper procedure and over a long practice churches and pastors have found them to be wise and constructive, it is a part of wisdom and common sense for a pastor to consider such methods rather than feel that "everybody is out of step except Johnny."

Major divisions have arisen during the past fifty years in several denominations over doctrine or social issues. Such places ethical demands upon the senior pastor and the church leadership of a denomination to lead their congregation to study the issues and together decide what position the church will take in the controversy. This is usually both divisive and traumatic. In personal conversation, group discussion and congregational deliberation, Christian love and courtesy in manner and speech should be demonstrated. Even though brothers and sisters should have differences in opinions and conclusions, they may still by the Holy Spirit respect and love each other.

The church has certain obligations toward the denomination that only the pastor can perform in their behalf. I refer to leading revivals and conferences, teaching study courses, presenting missionary causes, and attending conventions. The church should prayerfully allow the pastor to participate in these activities so that he feels he goes with their blessing. An alert pastor will discover new ideas, look at his work with a better perspective, do some much needed study, or enjoy very valuable relaxation. Not infrequently he accomplishes much more for his local ministry during the interlude off the field than he could have possibly done had he stayed home. The principle of unselfish service brings compensations here. What moral right does a church have to expect outside help for revivals or training schools unless they are willing to share the same?

Some pastors project their programs and the influence of their activities into the lives of other churches by bulletin exchange. Often a good word from one community will stimulate zeal and enthusiasm in another. This is a Pauline method. If you do quote from another pastor's bulletin and you know the source, it is ethical to give credit for the source.

Working with the Director of Missions
or Denominational Coordinator by Whatever Name

The minister should encourage and assist the local Director of Missions. Many times he has a thankless task. He works in difficult areas and often doesn't see the fruit of his labors. He is usually both overworked and underpaid and therefore harassed by personal problems of how to do all he should do and operate on a shoestring. He is often lonely. He cannot play favorites and therefore may avoid a needed intimate fellowship with pastors on the field.

Sometimes the coordinator may not have had the educational privileges enjoyed by many of the ministers. He may need books. He may not have adequate office space or equipment to do efficient work. Ministers should seek to understand and help remedy any deficiency by giving fellowship, encouragement, genuine interest and active support to him and his work. The pastor should seek to enlist his church in giving worthy and adequate financial support. He can give attention to the achievements of the missionary and see that proper recognition and commendation is made.

The church deserves to know of area missions work and may be informed by reports in the church bulletin. The coordinator should be invited to speak occasionally to the larger churches. One may argue that he needs to be spending his time with weaker groups, but the Director of Missions needs the contact with the stronger groups for his own sake, and the church needs this personal touch with him. Through the years I have observed considerable improvement in this respect, but there is still much room for more. Whatever else may be said, the Director of Missions should not be treated as a hired hand, although he is a servant of the churches.

Summary

In summary, concerning all minister-to-minister relationships, it can well be said that we should respect each other as persons, respect the contribution that each has made to the community, respect the abilities of each other in terms of meeting human need, and cultivate friendship on this basis.

The church has an obligation to the whole denominational program of which it is a part, and only the personal influence and effort of the pastor will suffice in fulfilling some of this obligation. This, too, involves cultivating a sympathetic appreciation for the work and place of all other churches, no matter how small or poorly equipped they may be. They are God's churches, and the fellow ministers, if in the will of the Lord, are the spirit-appointed under-shepherds. They have their problems and their opportunities and need the moral support of a stronger spiritual unit to encourage and fortify them. Some may have an inferiority complex or a defeatist attitude. Some need to be taught the way of the Lord more perfectly. When we love them first and let them know it by our Christlike attitudes, then they will seek our help and listen to our counsel.

9.
THE MINISTER AND THE WEDDING

Marriage has always been a social institution, and in most cultures it is a religious institution. In early times when there was no state license required, the priest or minister might determine who should be married. Public announcements were made over a period of time, and if there was no objection and the marriage was in keeping with the laws of that specific church, the minister would usually marry the couple.

In our contemporary culture, the state decides who has the legal right to marry. Laws concerning age, parental consent if under a certain age, health, waiting period and in some cases, and economic responsibility are some of the considerations. Generally speaking, it is the individual's right at a certain age, but there are still legal restrictions.

Some denominations have church laws and requirements for marriage. They may involve the marriage of a divorced person or certain other considerations that put the minister in the position of a judge as to the validity of a marriage or a person's right to marry. However, many denominations have no such rules, and in a church governed by the congregation the matter is essentially left up to the minister.

The Minister's Decision

This boils down primarily to the minister's attitude about divorce and the marriage of individuals who have been divorced. There are a number of stances that are taken.

1. Many young ministers determine that they will never marry anyone who has been divorced, and they usually hold to this conviction until they really have to face the issue by some divorced member of the congregation confronting the pastor with the question, "Will you perform my wedding ceremony?"

2. Some take the position that they should marry anyone who presents them with a license from the state. These have no formal rules to follow.

3. Another position is to examine each case on its own merits. This makes the minister a judge. Some say, "I will marry only the innocent party in case of divorce when the divorce has been granted on the grounds of adultery." Others raise questions about the legality or validity of the first marriage, particularly if it was between non-Christian people.

4. Others try to make the decision on the basis of being redemptive. The one who takes this stance will say to the couple, "Yes, I will perform the ceremony, but first of all, let's have premarital counseling sessions just as we do

for those who have never married." During these sessions the purpose primarily will be to see if some hang-ups from the first marriage should be resolved before entering into the second experience.

The pastor who plays God and marries the couple on behalf of God and the church is, in my judgment, being quite presumptuous. Only the couple themselves can know if they have really committed themselves to each other in marriage.

Marriage and Divorce – Remarriage

Marriage is a commitment leading to a total way of life, a shared partnership in all of life. It is this intimate life and love of two persons that leads to their natural expression of sexual union. The physical act of marriage is not marriage itself. The marriage license is more than a legal consent to a contract for sexual activity.

Christian marriage occurs when two people, male and female, covenant to give themselves to each other in agape love, thus sanctifying their erotic and companionable needs. The consummation of the marriage in sexual intercourse becomes symbolic of the uniqueness of their loving and sharing relationship. We have to understand, too, that sexual infidelity is far from being the only thing that can wreck a marriage. So there are a number of perplexing questions that a minister must face as he works through his own concepts of what makes a marriage and when a marriage is broken. It would seem from I Cor. 7:12-17 that Paul suggests that divorce is permissible on the grounds of the desertion by the unbeliever. It would also seem that Jesus may have allowed for divorce on grounds of sexual infidelity. The idea of separation without divorce was unknown both to the Jew and to the Greek. Further, neither Jew nor Greek ever questioned the right of remarriage following divorce. Indeed a divorce decree in the Jewish culture ended with the statement, "that she may marry whomsoever she will." Could it be that this explains why the right to remarry is not mentioned by either Jesus or Paul?

We are all aware that the divine norm for marriage was a monogamous relationship for life. But just as people sin and fail in other areas, some fail in this area. The grace of God always redeems and restores those who fail to meet the standards that God has set. In the New Testament grace has the final word. A minister charged with interpreting the mind and attitude of Christ to others must be sure that his own attitude is Christlike. Jesus did not condone sin; he did forgive sin and taught that those who were forgiven were in God's presence as though they had not sinned. He further taught that Christian forgiveness should be unlimited, and it is only from this point of view that some ministers can take their stance. In my opinion *realized forgiveness* on the part of the couple being married is the theological or biblical basis for marriage of those who have been divorced.

By being redemptive in the premarital counseling experience without being judgmental, the pastor may discover how persons formerly married previously faced the issues of marriage. It will not be his purpose to open old wounds or press for sordid details but to discover whether or not they have really satisfactorily handled the deep emotional trauma of a former experience.

More on Premarital Counseling

Ministers have often been guilty of deploring marriage breakdowns without any effort whatever to do preventive maintenance. This grievous sin of omission continues to wreck havoc in the homes of the members. Family Life Education should be a continuing program in any church. We now have many resources to aid our people in preparation for marriage.

For sixty years, to my knowledge, some pastors have attempted premarital counseling, but it has usually been too brief, hurried and superficial. It is my studied opinion that an ethical pastor will take this seriously. In four to six hours with the couple (an hour at a time) he can discuss with them the adjustments they will face: social, physical, economic, and spiritual. He will raise questions as to their expectations of marriage and of each other. He will discuss roles, values, communication patterns, dealing with conflicts, influence of their family backgrounds on adjustments, budgeting of money and time for each other, to mention a few considerations. He may make a check-up appointment for a dinner date six months following the wedding. Without special training in counseling, the concerned pastor can, with the aid of a few well chosen books digested and restudied, prepare himself for this part of his rose garden of pastoral care.

I submit it is unethical for a pastor, either by ignorance, fear, or the pretext of not having time, to abdicate this responsibility for premarital counseling. It is refreshing, indeed, to receive a letter written by a couple on their twenty-fifth wedding anniversary expressing appreciation for premarital counsel given them prior to the wedding day.

The Movement of the Wedding

Preparation for the wedding takes into consideration church policies as to the use of the church property and scheduling of wedding and reception and other matters.

In the premarital counseling session there will be some discussion about the wedding itself, looking toward the rehearsal. The janitor will be alerted and other involved staff members will be instructed. The license will be examined and proper official papers will be signed at rehearsal time.

In some areas today, someone other than the minister, often called a bridal consultant, directs the rehearsal. The minister should have an understanding with the bride as to his responsibility. He should let it be understood that while another may direct the movement of the service, he is definitely in charge at the *church altar*.

The rehearsal itself is confined primarily to what is called the movement of the service: the place of the music, the processional, the position of the wedding party at the altar, the opening address, and any desired congregational participation. As the wedding ceremony begins there may be a challenge to the audience, which is a modern way of issuing the bans. In earlier times, announcements were made in advance to see if someone knew why a couple should not be married. In some church ceremonies today, the question is asked the couple, "Do either of you know of any impediment that would hinder you from being united to each other in the bonds of matrimony?" The modern way of issuing bans has become simply a ministerial custom, and many ministers never ask this question. I really doubt the ethics of asking such a question in our time. I cannot recall ever asking it except in the beginning days when I was using a printed ceremony. I would encourage young ministers to carefully think through the wedding ceremony and prepare and memorize their own.

In the movement of the service there are other experiences reflecting traditions and custom even from ancient times. It is assumed that there has been an engagement or what the scriptures call an espousal. Now they come to make mutual promises and give expression of their willingness to take each other as husband and wife. There is giving of the woman in marriage by her father, in most instances. In certain ancient cultures and church traditions the father gave his daughter to the church, that is, to the minister, who in turn gave her to the man. Again, the philosophy of the minister about marriage will have something to do with whether or not he receives her from the father or the groom receives the bride from the father. Whoever receives her, receives her hand from the father, so the question is really whether the minister marries the couple or performs the ceremony. Most ministers would prefer to say, "I perform the ceremony."

To continue the movement, there is the plighting of the troth, the pledging to each other with the ring, the affirming of the ring or statement about it which is another way of blessing the ring as some early church fathers did. This is usually followed by a wedding prayer and the minister's pronouncement that the couple has taken their vows and by the authority vested in him by the state as a minister of the gospel, they are lawfully married husband

and wife. Often, they kneel for the final benediction.

In a double wedding, it is customary for the older girl to be married first even though the vows are taken almost simultaneously.

Most marriage manuals will not say anything about the nuptial kiss. But when it is done with taste (no pun intended), it can be a very meaningful part of the ceremony for the couple. This kiss of affirma- tion or commitment may only be done appropriately at this time.

Some ministers congratulate the couple before they leave the church altar. The recessional follows. The minister stands in his place until the mothers and perhaps the grandmothers are escorted from the chapel.

At the premarital counseling session, whatever service movement the minister is accustomed to and needs to insist upon must be worked out with the couple. There may be some variations. Many couples today are asking to write their own vows. Some ministers will permit this; others may not. Others will permit it after looking at the vows to see if they are in keeping with both scripture and tradition.

Some musically talented couples have been known to sing their vows to each other. There are a number of methods that may be used to create a special spirit of worship. A church wedding should be one of worship and joy and celebration as well as commitment.

Home Dedication

Some couples desire to have a home dedication service before they leave the church and following the wedding itself. Here is one way to do it:

As the couple turns to the minister, following the lifting of the veil and the nuptial kiss, the minister addresses the couple using the man's first name and the woman's first and married name: _____ and_____, do you desire that the home you are establishing be a Christian home? It is your purpose to dedicate it to the highest ideals of Christian homemaking, and do you desire, as you have given yourselves each to the other in marriage, now to give yourselves through your homelife to God?

(We do.)

In keeping with this desire, therefore, do you purpose to read your Bible and pray daily, to seek God's will for all your home relationships, and if your home should be blessed with children, do you resolve to make use of all the helps that God has given you in family religion through your church, that you may rear those entrusted to your care in the nurture and admonition of the Lord?

(We do.)

89

I charge you, therefore, in the sight of God and these witnesses to keep your torch of faith well-lighted and with the help of the Holy Spirit, who sanctifies the home with His presence, to recognize Christ as the head of your house, the unseen guest at every meal and the silent listener to every conversation.

> May nothing evil cross your door
> and may ill-fortune never pry
> about your windows: May the roar
> and the rains go by.
> Strengthened by faith, the rafters will
> withstand the battering of the storm;
> Your love, though all the world grow chill,
> will keep you warm.
> May peace walk softly through your rooms,
> touching your lips with holy wine,
> til every casual corner blooms into a shrine.
> And though your sheltering walls be thin,
> may you be strong to keep hate out
> and hold God and love within.

(Couple kneels for prayer)

Prayer: We thank Thee, Heavenly Father, that in Thy perfect wisdom Thou hast ordained the family relationship and dost assure to all who keep Thy commandments the assistance of Thy grace and the enduement of Thy spiritual power, that they may ever please Thee, and possess the inheritance promised to them that love Thee. Bless the home that _____ and _____ today establish. May it be a sanctuary where their love will find fullest expression and a place where their hearts secure safe refuge from the stormy conflicts and anxious cares of life. Mindful of Thy goodness, we do now rejoice before Thee as the giver of every good and perfect gift, and the source of all our happiness, God over all the blessed forever, in the name of Jesus Christ our Lord.

(Without Amen and with couple still kneeling):

Soloist sings Malotte's "Lord's Prayer."

Couple then rises and the wedding recessional proceeds as rehearsed. The home dedication is not rehearsed, though the wedding participants should be made aware of it.

Home Weddings

Home weddings are more simple, but it is often difficult to find proper places to stand during the ceremony. If there should be music, one must consider the position of the instrument, the size of the home and the expected number in the company. Home weddings may be in good taste and a worshipful experience. The same may be said for a wedding held in the minister's home, though it must be much more simple as one should not impose any extraordinary kind of hospitality upon a minister's wife. At the church study, there is usually no one present except the couple and the minister.

State Laws Vary

In some states a minister may not be authorized to perform weddings when he first moves into the state. It depends on laws concerning residence and authorization. In some states it has been necessary for the couple to be married in the same county in which the license was issued. In most states they must be married in the same state in which the license is issued. The minister needs to acquaint himself with the laws of his area through the local circuit clerk's office. Some states authorize only *ordained* ministers to perform weddings; other states will also authorize *licensed* ministers to do so. Usually the language is interpreted to mean that the minister must have the highest credentials in the denomination served.

The Minister's Dress for the Wedding

The minister should learn whether the wedding is to be formal or informal and how the wedding party will be dressed and how they prefer that he dress for the occasion. One of the simplest ways is for the minister to wear a clerical robe with clothing underneath that will be appropriate for the reception following. If he should have formal wear and the others are dressed formally, it would certainly be appropriate for him to do the same. Most couples do not desire the minister to rent formal wear for a reception, but it may be advisable that they rent appropriate attire for the wedding for him.

The Wedding Reception

Some ministers hesitate to attend wedding receptions if they think alcoholic drinks are to be served. However, one is under no obligation to participate in the refreshments. Usually, a thoughtful host will have two punch lines. Some feel that participation in such events would be a compromise of conscience. Others feel that they can exercise some influence over the people by attending. Usually one does not have to face this question. However, one may wonder about declining an invitation to a wedding reception because liquor is being served if he dines at restaurants where alcoholic beverage is offered him with the question, "Do you care for a cocktail before dinner?" He may have to face the question of whether he can be comfortable with a coke glass or some non-spiked punch in his hand while others are holding liquor glasses.

Expenses

In event he will have some unusual expense, it is better for him to have an understanding as wedding plans are being made. If it is advisable for him to go some distance by plane, for example, he may say to the couple, "Do you want me to fly?" He may ask, "Where will you arrange for me to stay?" Or he may say, "To avoid you any embarrassment, suppose I give you an expense estimate at rehearsal time." More ministers accept honorariums for weddings than for funerals. One may return the gift to the bride while another may turn the gift to his bride.

The Pastor and Wedding Presents

Some pastors simply have a practice of never sending wedding presents, but often the wife participates in showers to which she is invited. If would seem that some kind of standard gift from the pastor's family might be appropriate so that distinctions are not made.

Pictures and the Wedding

Most ministers do not approve of pictures being made during the wedding. Most of the pictures can be posed, except, perhaps, those of the couple coming out of the church or the bride starting down the aisle with her father. These can be made without obtrusion into the worship service.

Special Sticky Situations

Often the pastor is asked to perform a wedding when he knows the bride is pregnant. Or maybe she already has a child born out of wedlock. Or he is aware that the couple has been living together prior to the wedding. What should he do?

It has been rather traditional on the part of most ministers to perform the wedding ceremony and try to be as helpful as possible, acting redemptively. Surely it is not the time to preach or to be judgmental but to mediate the grace of God. There should be follow-up if at all possible in this home, probably for a long time.

What about an elopement or secret marriage? The age of the couple will certainly have some bearing on what he does here. He may exact a promise from them to announce their marriage to their parents or even ask permission to call the parents himself. In one instance where the bride's father was a minister, I suggested and then insisted she give him the opportunity to perform the ceremony and she agreed, much to the subsequent delight of all the family.

I have had a few experiences when the couple eloped and then decided they wanted to have a wedding in the presence of the family. I have conducted a Christian ceremony in the church in the presence of the family and thus honored the couple's desire to correct as much as they could the mistake they felt they had made. This has not been a second legal marriage but a church wedding following a civil ceremony. Whether the couple revealed their elopement has been their decision.

What of couples who present themselves while under the influence of intoxicating beverage, and one realized that perhaps they decided to get married after getting drunk? Most would suggest that they sober up and come back later. If the minister has the stance of always counseling with people before performing the ceremony, he will avoid this problem. Dr. Wayne Oates has called this "the confrontation and therapeutic approach," thinking primarily of divorce, but the whole concept of premarital counseling is valid for any pastor. If a couple is not willing to deliberately and prayerfully enter into such a relationship with the pastor, perhaps he would be wise to suggest that he would prefer not to have a part in the ceremony.

10.

THE MINISTER AND THE FUNERAL

"Comfort ye, comfort ye, my people," exhorts the Old Testament prophet. One of the pastor's most difficult tasks is being God's representative at the most critical time of life – the loss of a loved one. It is a time for quietness, calmness and assurance. The pastor must be confident in his voice and in his bearing. There should be no brashness or loudness.

The Movement of the Service

"Let me explain to you the movement of the service," the funeral director said. "Let me show you where you are to stand," another remarked upon my arrive at the funeral home, "then we will go out this way...".

The movement of the funeral service is under the direction of the undertaker from the funeral home or house through the benediction at the cemetery. The pastor should understand this and plan with the funeral director for this movement to be appropriate. Some ministers go to the home of the family and accompany them to the church if the deceased is being brought from home to the church. Others go to the funeral home and have a time of prayer with the family before the procession leaves for the church. Others wait for the family at the church door. Usually this is done if the body is brought to the church earlier than the funeral hour. The pastor always precedes the processional. Some ministers read or quote scripture as they move down the aisle. Others simply walk in silence. The minister proceeds to the pulpit and stands quietly until the funeral director has seated the family. Then he may be seated, as may the others of the congregation who have stood during the processional.

The minister should think through his prayers and scripture. Hymns, if any, should be carefully chosen. Whether by choir, quartet, solo or congregation, they should not be a dirge, but rather songs of hope and celebration. Sometimes a favorite hymn of the deceased is chosen and consequently does more harm than good in tearing at the emotions of the family. More and more congregations are participating in the hymn singing.

The memorial service may have a few brief remarks, but one should avoid eulogy, especially an extravagant eulogy. The day of the funeral sermon is about gone. Some statements concerning the life of the deceased can appropriately be woven into statements the minister may make to individualize the service. The person's life has spoken more loudly than any message the minister may give. The message should be warm, comforting, hopeful, directed to the family and friends.

In event the burial service is to be private or there is to be a cremation as is becoming more customary, there should be some announcement at the conclusion of the service at the church or funeral home. Otherwise, the pastor may say, "The service will be concluded at the cemetery," or simply give a benedictory prayer.

The pastor should confer with the funeral director as to the movement from the church or funeral home to the cemetery. After the family has had their farewell with their loved one, it is very unwise for the casket to be opened. Sometimes this is done, however, when the body of the deceased is taken back to the old home cemetery, which may be some distance from where the deceased has lived. The wishes of the family should take precedence here, but often the result of opening the casket is to tear down the comfort that the minister has sought to give. Fortunately, the *viewing of the remains* following the service is becoming obsolete. If the casket is kept open prior to the service, it should be closed before the family takes their places at the church or funeral chapel.

The Burial

In the movement from church to cemetery, the clergy precedes all but the directing undertaker's funeral car. It is customary for the pallbearers who wear hats to remove them and also for the minister to walk with his head bare. If the weather is cold or inclement and the undertaker does not suggest it, the minister may say to the pallbearers, "Keep your hats on, gentlemen."

Another tradition that is rapidly passing from the scene is the committal service which is a part of the English Lutheran tradition. Though once objected to by John Wesley, it has been included in the Methodist Manual. There seems to be no special objection to it except for the clause "ashes to ashes and dust to dust" and the practice that some of the funeral directors use in throwing dirt down on the coffin. When this service is used, however, petals of flowers are usually strewn rather than dirt. Many ministers of the evangelical tradition substitute the use of the Lord's Prayer or the Twenty-third Psalm at the graveside and include something of the committal service language in their own prayer and benediction.

Following the benediction, a comforting word is said to the bereaved at the graveside, and they are escorted back to their cars. The minister should leave the cemetery as soon as appropriate. It is usually not the place for visiting, but community custom, the distance from the place of the funeral service to the cemetery and other considerations may dictate tarrying a bit. Surely, this is not a place for levity or boisterousness.

Home Funerals

The minister should arrive close to the appointed time, see the family briefly and have prayer with them and then continue with the service. He does the best he can to stand where he can be heard, if not seen, by most of the people gathered. One must be prepared to deal with hysterics. Some family member or friend may *fall out*. This calls for control and an atmosphere of peace on the part of the minister. If the situation seems to be getting out of hand, he may suggest that the person be moved outside so the service may continue. Such a suggestion made within the hearing of the hysterical person will usually help them regain poise quickly as they do not want to miss the service.

In a service, the movement is just as important. The service should not be hurried but should be very brief and just as reverent.

Other Considerations

There should be some understanding with the undertaker concerning the hour of the service as well as other considerations such as the place of a fraternal order, honorary pallbearers or military funerals.

Sometimes a minister is called upon to conduct a memorial for one whose body is not present. This is a time for remembering and paying tribute. A printed order of service may be appropriate with a brief biographical sketch of the person being memorialized. In event of a fraternal order or military service, the pastor should have the exact understanding of what is to be done and when and be sure that these plans fit appropriately with the whole service, and certainly with the consent of the family. Sometimes groups move in and take over without the family's consent, unduly prolonging the service. The pastor should feel free to express his feelings on behalf of the family and insist that their wishes be observed.

Shortly after the service, he should telephone or visit in the home. If there are out-of-town relatives visiting, he may want to speak with them briefly, but his contact at this time should be short. The day following, he should check back by telephone if at all possible and continue to do so periodically as time goes on. Remembering that other friends and some family members will be more apt to forget as time passes. It is in their hours of loneliness when the presence of a comforter is needed most. Without creating undue dependency, the pastor will stand by until the member can adequately cope.

Special Situations

When you are asked to assist in a service, you should find out exactly what you are to do and when. When you ask another to assist, give him the same information. He should also be instructed about the movement of the service.

When you learn of the death of another pastor's member before he does, what do you do? Perhaps you have been in the hospital at the time or some member of the family is a part of your church. First of all, you should see that the pastor is properly informed even if you have to call him yourself, explaining how you got the information. Give him time to minister to the family first, in event you feel obligated to go also. Then when you go, bow out as promptly and as gracefully as you can. If you should be called upon to assist in the service, proper protocol should be observed by the pastor extending you the invitation. You, in turn, when learning that your church member wants another person to participate in a service, would express understanding of their feelings and offer to contact the fellow pastor.

What of special cases, such as burying one who has been murdered or has committed suicide? What about multiple deaths by accident or the death of a very prominent person? All of these circumstances add to the tension of the experience, but in the main the principles already discussed should be observed. Surely it is not the time to preach a sermon on judgment or even make an evangelical witness except indirectly. The message should be given to the living in terms of comfort, grace and strength.

Theology at Funerals

One should be very careful about the theology preached at funerals, such as ascribing everything to the will of God. It could be that the deceased played the fool and brought on his death. So his going *before his time* could not be blamed on God. Surely everything is in God's directive will or His permissive will. But much of what God permits He does not direct or inflict.

Neither is it the time to try to answer perplexing questions, even unanswerable ones such as "Why me?" "Why did this happen to us?" It is a time for the minister to proclaim without apology and with conviction and hope that "nothing can separate us from the love of God which is in Christ Jesus."

Coping with Grief

Perhaps it would be appropriate here to make a few observations concerning the pastor's ministry in helping others cope with their grief. Some pastors are mere professionals and of little comfort. For several years I played the role but didn't really have compassion – perhaps for two reasons: (1) my personal inexperience with grief, and (2) the fact that I had never thought seriously of my own mortality.

Returning from a funeral one day, I asked myself, "What do you really think about death? Now what you preached back there, does it really coincide with your belief?" For several weeks I read and reread Bible passages and books on grief, heaven and eternal life and thought about it. It was only then that I came to grips with my own inevitable demise without irrational fear. (I think most people have some dread of the unknown.) After this, I feel that I became a better comforter.

Feeling a sense of finality and fear in the presence of pending death of a church member, some pastors, as do others, even some family members, find their visits less frequent and shorter as the member approaches the final hour. Surely the pastor should avoid this because he has a ministry to the dying one as well as to the family.

Mrs. Hood, who had a brain tumor, asked, "Pastor, you are going to stay with me through this, aren't you? You know I'm not going to get well. Will you be with me all the way to the end?" As many other ministers have responded, I replied, "Yes, I will walk with you as far as I can, and then I will place you in the hands of the One who will go on through the valley with you to the other side."

The pastor should understand the grief process that is a part of all separation experiences from the little griefs, as the loss of a pet, to the grief experience in the loss of a loved one. The cycles, or stages, of grief are given various names by the specialists. These do not always occur in the same order. Usually one suffers first the numbing, chilling effects of *shock*. This may come when the doctor says, "It is terminal."

Denial usually comes next. "It's not true! It can't be happening to us – to him – or her." And the bereaved goes to the cemetery to visit the grave in an attempt to hang on to the belief that it didn't happen and later on, just to pay tribute to his or her memory.

Rejection or the feeling of being rejected may follow. He died! "What more could I have done?" I failed. "I wish I had spent more time with him/her." Rejection may be coupled with guilt.

Anger is often a part of grief. "Why me?" "What is God punishing me for?" Mad at God, the doctor, the hospital and the minister! I have had people beat me on the chest and curse God. In earlier days, I tried to defend God; now I merely try to defend myself. One usually will forget what he said when he was beside himself in grief. The minister should never use this to berate the person or make him feel more guilty, nor is this the time for a theological discussion.

Catharsis may be a part of working out grief. Some men have been conditioned not to express grief or hurt by shedding tears. "Now, now!" they were told as they were picked up and brushed off after a fall, "Big boys don't cry." But big *men* do, and most pastors are really big men, too. As Russell McIntire, my one-time associate, observed, "It doesn't hurt to show your heart." Bernard Clairvoux said, "I have sinned in that the well springs must come open, the tears must flow. It is the way God has allowed to wash the soul in the agony of grief."

The catharsis may be in telling the story over and over again, losing a little of the cutting edge each time, thus helping the healing process.

But after acceptance there comes *pining*, the wishing for the good things that once were. Fear, isolation, bewilderment, loneliness – all are parts of the cycle.

Depression is an inevitable part of the process. Either mild, moderate or severe, depending upon the combination of present circumstances and how well we have been taught to handle the separation experiences of the past. We all have cycles of ups and downs, but the grieving person may suddenly feel low and depressed to the point of despair. Depression may be masked for a time by an extreme *high*, and friends may say, "My, he's taking this well," but the mood swings back to *low*, and it hits hard.

We should remember that the episodes of pining or searching, followed by depression, may recur and usually move in cycles, but with less frequency and intensity of emotional impact as time goes on. So the pastor, knowing this, may caution the member not to be overwhelmed by a feeling of "here I go again" when there is a letdown. These experiences usually come around anniversaries, birthday, weddings anniversaries, Christmas and date of death or funeral. It is well to remind the member that "this, too, shall pass."

Some people suffer delayed grief. One seems to manage very well at the moment but after several weeks is found reacting as though the funeral were yesterday. Among the signs of delayed grief are:

1. Depression – The grieving person may become depressed and lose interest in life.

2. Self-pity – Some go through stages of self-reproach, self-pity and self-punishment.

3. Apathy – They complain that no one needs them and cannot be motivated into social interaction.

4. Over-dependency – They suddenly lose their ability to make life decisions.

5. Compulsion – They become overly demanding of themselves, others, or both.

100

6. Lack of emotion – Some develop a state of emotional flatness that may even be reflected in their facial features.

The pastor understanding these processes will help in the coping with grief in such a manner as to allow the grief to be worked through without a neurotic clinging to the deceased. There comes a time when we must let the dead be dead with thanksgiving for the joy in the good times. We accept the fact they are no longer with us and affirm our intention of reorientation of life without their physical presence.

The pastor will do well to hold a three-to-six hour seminar on grief at least once a year and be sure to include the older children. You will then minister to all ages as your statements will have to be simple enough that the adults will understand, too. No reflection on our intelligence, but preachers have a tendency to be philosophical.

11.
THE MINISTER AND . . .

Ministerial Dress

In the liturgical churches proper dress is prescribed with a distinctive garb. This prescription may be by tradition and custom or by regulation. This distinctive garb of the clergyman is always correct. However, in non-liturgical churches the minister is not quite so fortunate. About sixty years ago most ministers would wear a dark blue or gray suit when out among the people. This was the occasion for a remark by a Methodist minister who always wore sport clothes on Saturday as he walked around the town square. When met by one of his peers in *proper ministerial attire* he would say, "Long about this time of the week the devil just gets the best of me, and I find myself dressing like this."

In non-liturgical churches the pulpit gown has often been a part of the Sunday morning costume in the North and East and is now more prominent in the South. Southern clergymen a few generations ago would often wear a formal morning costume characterized by a black cutaway coat tailored in a plain styling with trousers of the same cloth or striped, either black and gray or black with fine white stripes. The other accessories were appropriately matched. However, in our day the attire for the morning service in most non-liturgical church is a two or three piece suit, depending on styling at that time.

A minister's dress should not be conspicuous enough to call attention to himself or his clothing. This might be a detriment to worship and cause the people to forget the message. Remembering one noted evangelist, I cannot recall his messages at all. I do not remember whether or not he was a good preacher. I do remember his red socks. I believe most ministers would rather be remembered for something more than that.

While clothes do not make a man, clothing and appearance reflect his personality. He does not need to dress expensively to be well-groomed. Cleanliness is essential in both his person and attire. Attention should be given to details and coordination. If he is one who does not have good judgment along this line, hopefully his wife will. His clothing store salesman can surely help in the coordination of his outfits. Some men are meticulous in their attention to certain kind of details and forget others such as hair grooming, finger nails, or polished shoes. Again, community customs and prevailing standards will in a large measure dictate how a minister dresses. Surely he will feel free to wear the same type clothing others do on informal occasions and while doing physical labor, and while he should feel free to assert his individuality, he should be careful not to be to eccentric in his dress.

When the minister receives an invitation that includes his wife, it is proper and considerate for him to ask the host or hostess about attire. This will put the wife's mind at ease, and since this is important to her, surely it will be important to him.

The Minister's Library

The minister's library may reflect his theological stance and the people he has learned to rely on in his study; or it may be simply for show. He may not have the working tools to do intensive Bible study. The books he has on the shelves may reflect too specialized study and consequently, hobby preaching. Some people would call it *grooved* preaching. Others say, "He's in a rut."

Some become buyers of many books and readers of few. They are always going to get around to reading this or that. Someone has said that the periphery of one's ignorance is determined by the circumference of his knowledge. All of us have to do specialized thinking and study to carry out the injunction to be "men who have an understanding of the times and to know what Israel ought to do." This demands a great deal of reading and a well-balanced library. Normally speaking, if the pastor is well-read, the flock will be well-fed.

On Making a Will

One who teaches the stewardship of possessions must surely include provision for the possessions that he may accumulate during his lifetime or which may come to his estate at his death. Therefore, it is unethical to teach or preach stewardship without teaching the concept of Christian will-making. The minister does not have to be in the pastorate very long before he sees families divided and lawyers and the government coffers enriched simply because one failed to make a will. Surely in this area, a minister could practice what he preaches.

The Minister and Public Functions

Often the minister is called upon to give the invocation or benediction at various and sundry public functions. Depending upon the nature of the occasion, the minister may either feel honored or used. Illustrations of what might be acceptable functional activities: certain school events, mayor's prayer breakfast, city council meeting, convening of the state legislature, supreme court memorial service, dedication of a public building, public school commencement or the dedication of a business of one of the members. Prayer for a candidate in a partisan political campaign might not be acceptable unless one wants to identify himself specifically with the candidate or that particular political party. To illustrate: There were two political faction in a major political party of one county. The gubernatorial candidate for one of these factions was coming to town. A deacon, who was chairman of the committee, asked the pastor if he would lead the opening prayer at the rally. The pastor declined. The deacon said he respected the pastor's desire to be nonpartisan. A week later he was asked to lead the prayer at the other candidate's rally. He again declined. Still later he was asked to lead the prayer to launch the campaign of a local man for United States senator. He asked the one extending the invitation, "Are both the political factions of this party supporting this man for senator?" The answer was in the affirmative, and the minister said, "Then I will lead the prayer for him."

What about other public utterances? One must recognize his responsibility for such as a citizen and also understand that it is most difficult to sever himself from his position as a minister and to speak only as a citizen in the community, though at times he feels that he must do this. There are other occasions when he can speak for his congregation, but he certainly must be sure of his ground when he takes this approach. There is a difference between a minister giving utterances concerning issues at a public function and speaking prophetically as a minister from his pulpit. The pastor must keep this in mind.

In terms of the political life, it is most important to respect minority viewpoints and those who hold different views. One should try to understand the reasons persons hold other views – that is, try to see from their vantage point. Though the perspective may be narrow, narrowness may beset the minister as well as others. Respect for personhood of those who differ with us is a highly ethical position.

The Pastor's Behavior toward Invited Guests

There are many opportunities for pastors to have guest speakers and preachers for regular services, a series of services, anniversaries, dedications, revivals, dinner speakers, seminars, conference leaders, to name a few. Here are some suggestions:

1. The invitation should be clear and specific as to time, date, place, what is expected of the speaker and how he will fit into the rest of the program. On receiving an affirmative response, it is courteous to reconfirm with appreciation and gratitude.

2. As time approaches, arrange hospitality details and apprise the guest of them. If he is driving to the church, he needs to be given explicit directions.

3. If the pastor is not going to be present, the guest needs to know who will be in charge of the service or program and other persons who will be involved.

4. He may need to know how he should dress if some formality is required or in keeping.

5. He should be correctly introduced. If the pastor does this, he should know the facts and stick to them. This information could be a part of pre-publicity materials the pastor requests following acceptance of the invitation.

6. Be considerate in not adding more details to his visit than those agreed upon unless he has consented prior to arrival.

7. Make a check of the lectern, lighting, public address system and seating arrangements.

8. If it is appropriate, the guest speaker's wife should be invited, but she should not be made to feel an obligation to accept.

9. Be sure to ascertain whether or not your guest has other schedules to meet preceding or immediately following your meeting and courteously give him the option of staying for other activities that may follow.

10. Be sure your treasurer has prepared a check for the guest speaker. The treasurer, the chairman presiding over the meeting or the pastor should hand it to him in private. Advance understanding should be made concerning honorariums and expenses with arrangements made to pay these promptly. "The treasurer is not here today" is a very poor excuse for your lack of consideration and failure in advance planning.

11. Don't apologize publicly for attendance, the weather, or conflicts that have arisen. These matters can be discussed privately. Do not take valuable time from the worship or learning experience of the people.

12. When the service is televised or on the radio, certain other details may need attention. Television may involve coordination of colors and movements. Details may have to be described to the guest. Most churches do not make a television production out of a church service, but some do. Everything is programmed and timed minutely. Each participant is told where to stand, sit or kneel.

13. Definite arrangements should be made for meal entertainment, opportunity for the guest speaker to rest in the afternoon if he is a Sunday supply, and other such courtesies that one will remember out of his own experience.

14. Whether the guest is a preacher on occasional assignment, evangelist or other speaker who will stay a few days, it is perhaps better for the person

to be kept in a motel or hotel. Though many people have the knack of making a person at ease in their home, there often seems to be a certain amount of formality that mitigates against relaxation. The opportunity for privacy is a most important consideration. If placed in a motel or hotel, it is very thoughtful to have a small basket of fruit in the room before arrival. A small arrangement of home-grown cut flowers would also add to his joy and feeling of warmth toward you and your people. If he travels by plane, it is thoughtful to provide a car while he is with you.

15. For meal entertainment of evangelists or other speakers it is appropriate to learn the preference of the guest. Some families find it difficult to entertain in the home due to work schedules. Some feel that one meal a day in a home should be the maximum, with the other meals eaten privately in a restaurant. Other churches bring food to the pastor's home or to the church dining room for the evening meal so the guest can eat as he may desire without feeling an obligation to the hostess that would tempt him to eat too much. Some groups find it convenient and desirable for members to invite the guest to eat with them at a restaurant. Most guests will welcome such an opportunity for fellowship and getting acquainted with church family people.

16. The guest usually needs some study time and prayer time. In the case of an evangelist, he may desire to visit prospects with the pastor or some church member.

17. It is advisable to make advance financial arrangements with an evangelist. Make clear what the arrangements will be, whether it will be a revival *love offering* or an honorarium that is agreed upon. Guest speakers usually consider this a subject that they should not approach, therefore it is the responsibility and the obligation of the pastor to suggest customary arrangements before an invitation is accepted. Since evangelists are dependent upon revivals for support of their families, it is absolutely imperative that they should know about this. Others ought to know as a matter of common courtesy.

The Preacher on Introductions of Other Preachers

People are interested in the background of a stranger coming to the church for some special event. Better to give the biographical facts in writing before the person arrives than to take up undue time relating personal history and activities.

One should be careful of facts. Do not give a man a title he does not have. Be careful of ascribing to him past positions he did not fill. It is easy to be mistaken, so one should carefully check his facts. If you make a mistake inadvertently and you are corrected by the brother, try to remember it. I have learned this the hard way. Even after being corrected, having a biographical sketch available but not in hand, I ascribed *in writing* certain faculty positions to an eminent brother that he never held. This was altogether my error, but some might have thought he had given out this false information. Those who really knew him would never think this. Nevertheless, my error was inexcusable and unethical. I should have remembered that he had previously corrected me and should have checked my facts. A little more care will save you much embarrassment as well as keep your behavior on the highest ethical level.

On Recognition of People in a Worship Service

Striving for warmth and good fellowship, most pastors have some method of recognizing visitors. Some ask the congregation to stand in honoring visitors. The ushers give a visitor's card to be filled out and dropped in the offering plate. Others ask visitors to stand or ask visitors to lift their hand. Some people like recognition. Others detest it. The pastor takes a chance of alienating or endearing.

Some churches use a "fruit basket upset" handshaking experience while singing some familiar song. To each his own! But it seems to me that very serious attention should be given to whether we are honoring persons or worshipping God. A warm, sincere *brief* word can be given with some method of visitor registration that takes little time and avoids any possible embarrassment of the timid ones.

The Ritual of Friendship used by some churches impresses me as an appropriate way to register and recognize visitors. The sheets (see sample) are on pads placed in the pew racks. There is room for ten names on one sheet. In the order of service there is included this statement: During the offertory everyone is requested to sign The Ritual of Friendship blanks found in the pew racks. Visitors may also wish to fill out a visitor's care found in the racks.

You will note that you get an attendance record of your *members* as well as the *visitors* in The Ritual of Friendship. At announcement time, which was at the close of the worship service in the church where I was visiting and picked up the sample shown on page 109, the minister expressed appreciation for the congregation's participation in the Ritual of Friendship and said, "We are indeed happy to have those of you who are visiting with us today and would remind you that when God's people come to His house, they come home."

What about the visit of some prominent person such as the mayor, the governor, or some denominational agency representative? Usually they would prefer not to be *limelighted* – that is, if they are present to worship. If the recognition is made to make the pastor look important because such a person has come to hear him preach or to stroke Mr. Prominence, perhaps recognition should be forgotten. Yet, there are times when the church members should know of the presence of the official for *their* sakes. So one must do what he feels he must do as long as he remembers that it is unethical to turn the sanctuary of worship into an ego-massage parlor.

RITUAL OF FRIENDSHIP

WESTMINSTER PRESBYTERIAN CHURCH
NASHVILLE, TENN.

1. EVERYONE IS ASKED TO SIGN THE SHEET.
2. AFTER EVERYONE HAS SIGNED, PASS THE SHEET BACK.
3. LOOK AT THE NAMES OF THOSE IN THE PEW WITH YOU.
4. GREET ONE ANOTHER AT THE CLOSE OF THE SERVICE.

NAME	MEMBER AT WESTMINSTER		VISITOR INFORMATION	
	YES	NO	HOME ADDRESS	HOME CHURCH

Denominational Methods to Move Ministers

In the free church tradition, when a pastor desires to move, he has four choices in addition to praying and asking for leadership.

1. He can notify the Church Minister Relations chairman of his denomination about it.

2. He can talk with other denominational leaders and indicate his feelings about a possible move.

3. He can speak with other trusted friends in the pastorate or with some lay people in places he has served.

4. Under certain circumstances he may make some direct approaches to church committees, although this is thought by many to be an unethical procedure.

One young pastor was told by a state executive secretary during a friendly chat that he had been recently contacted by a pulpit committee chairman regarding their need of a pastor. The executive secretary said, "You are going back through that town on your way home. Why not stop in and see the chairman *at my request* and learn whether or not they have called a pastor. Get acquainted with him and see what comes of it." The young pastor questioned if this would be an ethical approach, and the executive secretary replied, "Under the circumstances and with my requesting you to do this, I think it is perfectly ethical. If you find that they have someone under consideration, you will certainly thank him and bow out. If he is interested in talking with you further, then you can just see how the conversation goes." The young man took his advice, made the call, and within three weeks was the pastor of the church. The entire initiative was taken after his introduction by the chairman himself.

Usually the church seeks the minister rather than the minister seeking the church. It is considered ethical to let some of your friends know that you may be interested in a certain situation after it becomes open. Not before.

When the church seeks the minister, his response should be that of courteous consideration if he is at all interested in moving. It could be that there are some ethical considerations involved in his present location. Possibly he has not been with the church long enough, the church is in a building program or special financial campaign, or problems need to be solved before he leaves. His answer could well be: "Anytime any church committee desires to talk with me, I'm honored. I feel I must learn more about your situation just as you desire to learn more about me, so let us enter into a frank discussion with each other. If either of us desire to terminate the discussion, we can do so." This gives opportunity for pointed questions by both the committee and the minister.

Among the questions to be discussed are these (not listed in any particular order):

1. What type of church community do you have?

2. How is your present church program meeting the needs of your community?

3. What opportunity do you think there is for growth and development of the church?

4. What is the church budget? How does this reflect the potential giving of the congregation?

5. What of church polity? How are you organized?

6. What do you expect of your pulpit ministry?

7. What are your expectations of your pastor? Do you desire an 18-hour day or are you willing that he might have some time with his family?

8. How do you feel about your community relations as a congregation? Do you have a good reputation in the community?

9. What about your relationship with other churches and denominations?

10. What is the history of your church as to length of pastorates?

11. What are the cultural and economic levels of your congregation?

12. Is the church diverse or do you essentially reach only one socioeconomic group?

13. What about housing, salary and other considerations such as vacations, revivals, pulpit supply, conventions, social security, annuity, hospitalization, church-related automobile expenses, utilities, telephone at the pastorium, long distance calls made by the pastor, book fund, pastor's hospitality fund?

14. How are the church officers (deacons, elders, others) organized?

15. What kind of care-giving ministry does the church have?

16. What uniqueness is there about your church ministry?

17. What is the general attitude of the congregation? Conservative as to methodology? Is there a willingness to try new approaches or a desire to follow traditional patterns?

18. Is there any dirty linen that needs to be aired? That is, any recent split or serious dissension in the church for any reason?

19. What about sociological changes in the community? How will this affect the life of the church?

20. Does the church expect the prospective pastor to visit on the field with a so-called trial sermon?

21. What type of visiting on the field is acceptable in meeting church leadership, the church staff and others?

22. What staff does the church have? How does the committee feel about the efficiency of the staff? Are they satisfied to keep them on or is there a hidden agenda like the pastor having to be responsible for firing some staff member after the pastor arrives because the church does not have the courage to deal with the situation?

23. Does the church usually make a unanimous call? What is the policy if the call is not unanimous? Will they apprise the prospective pastor of this, giving him necessary facts on which he can base a value judgment?

24. Is there a job description for the pastor?

25. Will a copy of the church minutes dealing with the call of the pastor involve a contractual arrangement? That is, will it state all the conditions of the call?

26. Does the church have a constitution and bylaws? (The prospective pastor should examine these.)

Some pointers that might help:

1. Do not play the present church against the prospective church. Do not deal with two pulpit committees at a time. Do not allow bargaining.

2. Relate necessary facts to your own church people at the proper time.

3. Don't keep two congregations upset for an undue period.

4. Avoid the idea of taking *your* program to a new church field. No pastor knows what the new church needs until he has been on the field at least six months, usually longer.

On Going to a New Field

Some of the first visits one should make after moving to a new field will include:

Hospital Administrator

Doctors (as you can make the opportunities)

Funeral Home establishments

Welfare Department

County Health Department

News people

Radio and television station managers and programmers

City Hall

Police Department

Sheriff's Department

Juvenile Court workers and judge

Pastors of other churches (if they do not come to see you soon)

Bank officials (especially where the church does business)

Establishments that serve the church in some special way, such as printing, office supplies, heating and air conditioning.

While all these initial visits are time consuming, they may be used to say, "I appreciate the service you render to our people, and I just want to get acquainted with you to personally thank you and assure you of my best cooperation with you." Pay special attention to and get acquainted with the secretaries of these persons. They often hold the key to reaching them when you need them.

Exit Rules for a Departing Pastor

We quote with permission of the *Baptist Standard*, Dallas, Texas, this article by David Wilkinson.

When the time comes for a minister to leave, many churches and pastors discover that they don't know how to tell each other goodbye. As a result, the final weeks of a pastor's ministry often are unfruitful for both the pastor and the church.

Fred McGehee, career guidance consultant, believes those final weeks don't have to be ineffective and submits the following.

It's *very important* for ministers to know how to leave and for churches to know how to let them leave. We have too much movement in the ministry at the present time. Tenures are too short, and that's unfortunate.

However, in learning how to deal with closure – that is, how to close out a ministry more effectively – we may do churches and ministers the service of not having to do it as often. The minister, in the act of leaving correctly, may give himself the freedom to stay longer in his next pastorate. And on the other hand, the church will be left with a positive hope that the next pastor will stay longer.

Since it is usually the pastor who takes the initiative in leaving, he should also take the initiative in making the final weeks as effective as possible.

The pastor ought to make a brief sweep over his church roles and ask himself, "How will my leaving at this time influence these people?" When he does this, he's going to come across people who will be influenced in different ways. Some, for example, are going to feel really rejected by what he's going to do.

Others will be shattered. They've depended upon him in certain ways. He's in the process of going through certain important experiences in life with them, and these experiences and these times together are going to be interrupted.

In some instances the congregation as a whole may feel a sense of rejection.

If it is a very supporting kind of congregation, the church may feel as if its pastor is going on to bigger and better things. But in saying that, what does it do to them? It implies that their situation is both smaller and lesser, which in a sense is a personal putdown. So to lose a pastor is to receive a personal judgment.

The pastor can help by reassuring the church of its uniqueness and explaining that comparisons should not be made between the present situation and his future pastorate.

This will free the pastor to talk at a deeper than just theoretical level about what the will of God means in his life.

During the final weeks of his ministry, the pastor should also attempt to heal strained relationships with members who have reacted negatively toward him and with others who have been reluctant to respond to his efforts toward establishing meaningful relationships.

The former category often includes people who may have been antagonistic toward authority in general, but not necessarily toward the pastor as a person.

This means that the closure time is a time of supreme importance because the pastor is moving out of the authority role, and it may be that only under these circumstances will the antagonistic church member feel free to establish any kind of relationship with the pastor.

Properly saying goodbye to the children in the church is another area that is often overlooked.

The pastor certainly ought to consider the children. Many of them aren't going to understand why the pastor's children, who are their friends, are going to leave. And they aren't going to understand why this man who has been their pastor and Vacation Bible School leader and so forth, who has said that he loves them, is now going to leave them.

It is suggested that the minister go into the children's Sunday school classes and talk with them about why he is leaving in terms that they can understand.

The pastor can explain the meaning of the will of God at an interpersonal level, and it also helps him move into a friend-pastor role and build a bridge for the next pastor.

Properly closing relationships involved in the pastor's counseling ministry also is essential.

The minister usually knows about his move at least a month ahead of time, and he has made an ongoing commitment to his counselees. He needs to do everything in his power to stimulate growth in those last few sessions. Some counselees, for instance, may say some things they never felt free to say before since they know the pastor is leaving.

The minister should take care of necessary referral processes, and make sure that the referral is complete before leaving the community.

Consideration in the final weeks should also be given to the elderly, who may feel threatened by a pastor's move, and, of course, the minister should give attention to his own personal needs and to those of his family.

Once the move has been made, I suggest the minister write a letter to the church expressing thanks for its encouragement and cooperation and assurance of his prayers in its search for a new pastor.

Obviously, no minister can hope to accomplish all of these things before leaving a pastorate.

The individual can only do what he has the unique strength and ability to do. The important thing is that he feels he has taken the initiative to leave relationships on an upswing rather than a downswing.

The minister needs to realize that he can plan the way he wants a piece of work to conclude. He can choose for it to conclude on an optimistic, positive and redemptive note, or he can choose for it to conclude with possible pessimistic, destructive and antagonistic feelings.

He has a choice, but he's going to have to live with that choice for the rest of his life.

Dissension in the Church

What do you do when you have dissension among the members that centers around *you*? What do you do when some few vocal members want you to resign? More often than not, dissension is between factions in the membership, and the pastor is used as a scapegoat. In the church power politics during intervals between pastorates, the factions vie for leadership advantage. They, in turn, curry favor to get an ally in the new pastor. If not careful, he will be brought into an already existing division, all the while being told, "Yes, we were divided, but that has all healed."

Again, problems may arise that are of the pastor's own making. Most of us err at times in handling situations or dealing with persons. What should a pastor do when the prayer of those on more than one side is, "*My* will be done, O Lord"?

While serving as Director of Missions in Hinds County, Mississippi, for an eight-year period, I dealt with more than one hundred crisis situations in the churches, most of them centering around the pastor. Some church members can be most insensitive, vicious and cruel. One is reminded of the oft repeated story of the preacher who sought to comfort a pastor friend with Romans 8:31b: "If God be for us, who can be against us?" to which the troubled friend replied, "Deacons! That's who!"

We hasten to add that deacons are usually the pastor's strongest supporters and helpers, but some church leaders usually are in the forefront of the church division.

What to do? I make a few suggestions that may be helpful.

Don't panic. Don't precipitate the crisis. It has been a while in the making. If possible, let time work on the solution.

Pray for leadership of the Holy Spirit, especially that you may demonstrate the fruits of the Spirit: love, gentleness, peace, goodness, faith, patience and temperance.

Try to discover the *real* problem. With the aid of trusted leaders (and maybe some you wonder if you *can* trust), attempt to get at the heart of the matter. Has there been re-infection from an old wound? Does scar tissue need to be removed? Have you inadvertently reopened these sores?

Are there family problems of some of the leaders surfacing through misplaced hostility? I have observed that when church leaders are having trouble at home, they project their frustrations through church meetings and groups. Have you overextended yourself emotionally and physically and in your frustration or depression berated or whipped the congregation, building some triviality completely out of perspective? Kierkegaard once remarked upon leaving such a service, "I feel like I have been beaten to death by a flock of geese."

Have you offended someone by neglect through ignorance of a need? Through pressures of time? Or simply because they are difficult to get along with?

If you should discover any problem between you and some of the membership, try to work it out on a personal basis. In circumstances where you feel you may be taken advantage of, misquoted or misrepresented, then you should take some trusted neutral brother or sister along with you.

Don't let pride prohibit you from admitting mistakes and asking forgiveness.

Ascertain if there are compromises that should be made, not in matters of convictions but in areas of method or timing (and this is usually where conflict arises). I recall when I was convinced the time was right for us to take another step in a building program. Respected brethren disagreed with me, and I reluctantly gave in to their feelings. Two years later we made the step very successfully because we had waited. My timing was off; they were right, though I couldn't see it at the time and was quite disappointed with their low vision. It later was a joy to commend them on their good judgment.

Be careful not to create the impression that when people oppose you they are opposing the Lord. Each may be misreading the will of God. One can stubbornly insist on his being right and alienate others, including his friends. One pastor friend wrote me concerning a problem, concluding with the words, "I am dead right about this!" My one-sentence reply was, "You can be dead right and still be a dead duck." After allowing time for that to simmer with him, I tried to write a more helpful word.

Try to avoid bringing the matter to a church vote (such as a vote of confidence) unless that seems to be the only way to clear the air. Voting often magnifies the division instead of helping heal it.

If you feel in God's will that you should really move to another field, ask the church leaders to pray for His leadership, saying, "We are confident that God led us together. Now let us pray for His direction if we are to sever this relationship. God is not the author of confusion. If my work here is finished,

He has some place else. Let us pray that He will move me there."

Do not resign without a place to go unless you are forced to do so. I feel that a church acts unethically in vacating the pulpit without the pastor's having a place to go unless there are moral matters involved.

While in any dissension the pastor should remember that the cause of Christ is bigger than his personal interest. It is sometimes difficult to ascertain whether he should give in to a vocal minority. It might be better to exercise some New Testament church discipline and withdraw fellowship from obstreperous members. Such decisions must be prayerfully made in Christian love, seeking restoration before repudiation.

(Your denomination may have a suggested or adopted procedure for handling dissension. Eg., in one Presbyterian tradition this is the responsibility of the "ruling elders.")

On Surrendering Ordination Papers

In most Baptist denominations as well as number of others, the ordination of ministers is entirely up to a local congregation. No other ecclesiastical body has any control over them. Theoretically, therefore, the only group that can ask for the surrender of ordination is the church that called for the ordaining counsel and authorized the ordaining of the minister. This places an ethical obligation upon the minister. If he finds himself at variance with the doctrinal views he expressed and accepted at the time of his ordination, he should voluntarily surrender his papers. If he continues in the ministry, he should join the group that more nearly represents his new viewpoint. If the minister should decide that he was not really called to the ministry and that his preference or choice is to do some other work, it would seem only proper that he would surrender his ordination papers. We realize that this is seldom done, but it is surely the ethical thing to do.

One hesitates to suggest a course of action in the case of serious immoral conduct that becomes offensive or an embarrassment to the church or denomination, for it is difficult to know all the dynamics involved. No doubt there are circumstances in which the minister himself ought to seriously consider asking the church that ordained him to confer with him about the possibility of giving up his credentials. A great deal would depend on the nature of the circumstances, the repentant attitude of the minister and the redemptive attitude of the congregation as to whether or not his work and service could be positively salvaged for the future.

Women in Leadership

One shudders to think where the Kingdom work would be without the faithful women in the churches. Our missionary work, home and foreign, would be seriously curtailed, if even existent. Leadership in the church would be so crippled as to make ineffective the teaching and training ministry. Paul made an excellent suggestion when he said, "Help those women."

Some preachers seem to fear women. Others talk about them with a superior air. Many of the male chauvinist jokes told by preachers are a put-down on women.

In the four decades past, I have noted a decided change in attitude on the part of pastors toward *women's work*. It is not spoken of lightly so much today. More words of appreciation are being given. More avenues of professional service have been opening to women.

The question of women being set apart to some phase of the gospel ministry is coming to the fore in most all the major denominations. To some this is an incredible development. I suppose one of the reasons I have not been so perturbed about the recent events is that I remember a woman Baptist preacher of seventy years ago in north Missouri Southern Baptist churches. She, with her husband, co-pastored eight quarter-time churches, alternating the pulpit ministry month by month. The people were always delighted when Sister Smith came as she delivered "more powerful sermons" than Brother Smith. But some will say: "Just because it is being done doesn't make it right." To which I would agree.

However, the current situation should call each of us to study the whole question of call and ordination. In our culture, one wonders what Paul would say – or better, one wonders what Jesus would do. How is the Holy Spirit gifting persons in our time?

At whatever conclusion we may arrive, Christian ethics demands our respecting those who may have been "set apart" by some congregation as ones who could have had as valid a call as we male pastors feel we have had. While ordination is of some concern to the denomination in our Baptist mores, it is a responsibility of the local church.

One must observe that some women seem afraid of the freedom they have in Christ, which is real liberation, and they do not seem to know how to handle this freedom. The discerning pastor will offer guidance to the church in using the gifts (talents) of the women in the congregation in such a way that none will feel they are second-class members.

Refuting False Doctrine

There are varied opinions about minor doctrinal matters that are really of little consequence. Baptists differ in several matters but have not allowed them to be a cause for a breach of fellowship – for example, eschatology, particularly the second coming of Christ and premillennialism. This sentence was true in 1978 when the first edition of this book was written. During the years since, many of the "major denominations" have had controversies, and some divisions have resulted on *social issues*, such as race, world peace, human rights, church-state separation; *doctrinal issues*, such as creedalism, authority of scriptures, nature of God and creation; *political issues*, such as communism, democratic representative government or theocracy, where, as one remarked, "Everybody wants to be *Theo*" (Greek for God). Basically an examination of the dissension and division resulting in so much power play has brought more coercion to religious bodies with a consequent falling away and changing of denominational affiliation of clergy and members.

Bishop Harmon in his *Ministerial Ethics and Etiquette* published in 1950 avows: "There is no more reason for a minister to withdraw from his denomination because he cannot agree with it upon some minor question of polity or doctrine than there is for a wife to seek a divorce because she does not like the kind of necktie her husband insists on wearing."

Each person has to decide for himself what he considers major and minor. There are some issues about which the minister cannot conscientiously keep silent, and he is ethically bound to discuss them with his people. He must not allow what the New Testament calls *grievous wolves* to come in and destroy. He must contend for what he believes to be the faith once delivered. So when isms and cults appear, he will try to understand their teachings and point out to his people the errors in them according to his interpretation of the scripture. Failure to confront these false doctrines would do a rank disservice to his membership. It can be done positively without being on the defensive, thus protecting his flock from those who would confuse them.

The Pastor as Church Errand Boy

There are a number of tasks about a church that should be delegated to others. Some communities expect the pastor to do all janitorial service, unlock for meetings, turn off the lights, turn on the heat, fill the baptistery, mow the church lawn, take members to the doctor or welfare office, and many other chores. Often he may quite easily do these things. Some enjoy doing certain tasks, such as keeping the lawn – if the church has a riding mower! The impression should never be given that he is above any errands, especially in emergencies.

For reasons of involvement and responsibility, it is much better to delegate these tasks as a ministry opportunity to others. If made responsible, many members would be gladly accountable in these details, and the pastor may be free for matters more in keeping with his professional training. His serving as errand boy could be an unethical deprivation of privilege that members of the congregation would enjoy.

On Seeking Advice or Counsel

One of my professors defined *genius* as "the art of knowing where to go to get information when you need it." Consult the experts! The minister is consulted about many areas plainly out of his field of expertise. It is unethical to give an opinion without any real basis of fact. Facts are usually relatively easy to obtain. The minister should remember this when he needs help.

Important decisions must be made on the basis of all the facts you can get and *personal problems* should be resolved in the same way. Let's face it. We do have problems. God does not exempt us simply because we are ministers, nor do we have a hot line of direct word from Him. If one hears voices, he does have a problem!

The medical doctor, the Christian psychologist, the psychiatrist, the attorney, the banker, a consecrated common-sense-wise deacon, another minister – all of these are among those who can help us. One is stupid indeed not to take his problems to those who can help. One is arrogant, to be sure, if he is so puffed with pride that he cannot admit he ever has a problem and is foolish to blunder on without help when it is readily available.

Unfair!

It is not fair to give a lot of attention to the new mother and ignore the new father. It is not right to be empathetic with the wife in a marriage breakdown and not recognize the needs of the husband. It is inconsiderate to give your attention to a bereaved spouse and neglect to comfort and listen to the children.

It is unethical to cultivate some cliques in your congregation and overlook others. It is unloving to treat a wealthy member with such deference as to discount his personhood. Likewise, it is unloving to ignore the poor, the dirty, the ignorant. It is distasteful for a man of the cloth to shun the untouchables – the alcoholics, the divorcees, the welfare recipients, the shiftless and ne'er-do-wells. It is repulsive to see a minister curry favor with denominational people, politicians or others whom he feels might help him climb up the ladder of bigness.

It is not fair to wear a mask. Some of your people want to really know you! It is ethical to be yourself with all your strengths and weaknesses. All the time – be yourself!

What Do They Call You, Preacher?

Community custom, education of the people and temperament of the pastor will enter into this. After being given an honorary doctorate, one minister, evidently somewhat conceited, insisted that his wife call him "Doctor" even in the home.

Reverend is not a proper address unless the precedes it.

Rabbi (teacher) is the favorite term of the Jewish people.

Father is usually used by the Catholic membership.

Parson (the person) was rather widely used when the minister, because of education, leadership or both, was literally *the person* of the community.

Preacher is a rather informal address, and members usually use it as an affection term. This is probably a cultural hangover from the days when the rural minister *preached* on stated Sundays.

Pastor! This was my favorite term to be used by the members of the congregation. It suggests a shepherd ministry, loving care and concern.

Many church members prefer to address their minister as *doctor* when he has an earned or honorary degree. Many do not know the difference and confer degrees upon all ministers. The ethical minister will prefer not to accept his, but sometimes it is difficult to correct the *conferrer* without embarrassing him. One could say, "I appreciate the title, but I don't have the degree to go with it." Neither those who have earned them nor those who haven't should make a *big deal* of it.

Sister! Brother! Now that's a good title – as is appropriate.

Hey, You! may get attention, but it is not very respectful.

What about first names? This is becoming more common. Some pastors encourage first names to keep from the *pedestal* life, which is unreal and very lonely. Others feel that too much familiarity may result in disrespect for leadership and the prophetic ministry. The chief consideration here is respect for the person. If first names are used flippantly by children and young people, it could mean more respect than use of a title. The same could be said for older persons toward a younger minister.

The general attitude, tone of voice and other courtesies will reveal more than a name. In conversation with others, church members usually will refrain from referring to their minister by the first name. The minister has

121

no control over this, but one can set the example in reference to fellow ministers. Various community customs will influence the use of first names, as will the temperament of the person being addressed. Some are just not first name persons. Others are.

If the pastor has any preference about the name he is called, he should indicate it at the beginning of his work with a congregation. If someone is using his first name, it does not follow that he should use theirs. He may ask as we often do among friends, "What do you prefer I call you?" Or he may have someone say, "Will you please call me _____?" If one prefers to be called by his first name, he should especially make such a request.

What's in a name: It was reported that the name Maxwell House sold for 48 million dollars. Only the *name*! "A good name is rather to be chosen than great riches." As long as you are called by the name that stands for *you*, that tells who you are in personhood or relationship, you are being honored by that name as you desire to bring honor to it. In bringing honor to his own name, the Christian minister brings honor to the Name above every name!

EPILOGUE
HOW CHURCH MEMBERS SHOULD BEHAVE
TO BE THE MINISTER'S FRIEND

"Jesus calls us to be his friend and the friends of God."
William Barclay

"A friend loveth at all times."
Proverbs 17:17

"I no longer call you servants but friends."
"You are my friends if you do what I command you; Love one another."
John 15:9-15

"If anybody is caught in the very act of doing wrong, you who are spiritual, in the spirit of gentleness, must set him right; each of you continuing to think of yourself, for you may be tempted, too. Practice bearing one another's burdens, and in this way carry out the law of Christ." (Galatians 6:1 and 2, trans. C.B. Williams, Holman 1986).

As she awaited major surgery, Mildred told her minister that she had a simple faith, expressed in the children's song, "Jesus loves me; this I know, for the Bible tell me so." No wonder next to the hymn, "Amazing Grace," one of the most favored is "What a Friend We Have in Jesus."

A colleague once reportedly prayed in Congress:

"God, I pray that all Jews may come to know Jesus.

I pray that all Moslems may come to know Jesus, and

I pray that all Christians may come to know Jesus."

Jesus said, "I am the way and the truth and the life. No one can come to the Father except by me" (John 14:6). He didn't say that any particular doctrine or religion was the way, the truth, and the life. He said that He was. He came to show us the Father and how to serve and worship Him. He didn't say that it was by believing or doing anything in particular you could *come to the Father.* He said it was only by Him – by living, participating in, being caught up by, the way of life that he embodied. That was His way – *The Way*!

Worship God! Know Jesus and follow Him. The six-year-old closed his prayer, "Thank you, God, for whoever made you. I don't know who it is." At twelve years in a poem entitled "God" he wrote, "If it were not for God, I couldn't write this poem." Perhaps the often quoted, "There go I BUT for the grace of God," should be better said, "There go I BY the grace of God." To know and follow Jesus is to know the God of grace and God of glory.

Congregational Ethics
Living Together

The principles by which we should live in our interpersonal relationships are summarized in the Sermon on the Mount with its joyful beatitudes, usually translated *happy are we* or *happy are you*, but the beginning of these beatitudes ought to be, O, the blessedness. Oh, the joy of following Christ! In the days of the early church those who observed the life of these early church members exclaimed, "Behold, how these Christians love one another."

In most congregations there is usually a certain amount of civility and good manners toward each other. We're led to feel a very large percentage of professing believers are sincerely trying to be practicing the precepts of their faith. The Ten Commandments are held among many groups in the Christian tradition as foundational ethics. Add the Lord's Prayer and the Sermon on the Mount, and you have the basic ethics for most congregations, and we would not be writing such a book as this if these principles, properly understood, were really being practiced.

In my college freshman year I was shocked almost out of my chapel seat when the New Testament professor leading the devotional said, "Jesus broke every one of the Ten Commandments." Then following a brief pause, he added, "He broke them by superceding them." Whereupon he moved through the pertinent gospel passages to show how He superceded them. One's attitude and actions toward our congregational fellow members may serve as a barometer as to how well we are living and practicing the new standards Jesus set for us.

The summary is found in Matt. 5:21-48. To name a few, "Thou shalt not kill" is replaced with anger as the root meaning of the word that Jesus used. Anger in the heart and anger in the speech are equally forbidden. But the sin of contempt is worse. And Jesus says, "He who destroys his brother's name and reputation deserves Gehenna," the place where useless and evil things were destroyed.

We cannot be right with God until we are right with our fellowmen (Matt. 5:23-24). Get on good terms with those who oppose you (vv. 25-26). Act to remove any barriers. Do not allow any feuds to fester. Jesus, also, condemns the person whose using his or her eyes to awaken desire for a forbidden thing, something to stimulate, titillate, and excite the wrong desire. Further, one's word should be as good as his bond (vv. 33-37). We are to regard all promises as sacred, since they are all made in the presence of God. In Matthew 35:42 Jesus renounced the law of tit-for-tat (still very prominent in our world), because retaliation, however controlled and restricted, has no place in the Christian life. The Christian thinks not of his rights but his duties, not of his privileges but his responsibilities, and he will never think of his right to do as he likes but always his duty to be of help.

"Love your enemies," Jesus admonishes (Matt. 5:43-48). This passage describes essential Christianity in action. The word used for *love* is *agape*, which means the power to love those whom we do not like and those who do not like us. This is only possible when Jesus Christ enables us to conquer our natural tendency to anger, to bitterness, and to achieve goodwill to all people. But we are to do more. We are to pray for them. No one can really pray for another and still hate him. We cannot go on hating another person in the presence of God. This all may seem to be impossible, but our behavior patterns, our ethical relationships in our congregational church life depend upon everyone being perfect. Impossible? The word translated *perfect* is *teleios*, which means *an end, a purpose, a goal*. So a person becomes perfect when he realizes the purpose for which he was created. According the Genesis 1:26, we find God saying, "Let us make man (male and female) in our image and after our likeness." Male and female were created to be like God. God is love! The great characteristic of God is to love all, constantly seeking the highest good of every person. A person who cares the most for people is the most perfect person. The one thing that makes us most like God is the love that never ceases to care for people.

Other instructions of Jesus from the Sermon on the Mount concern commitment in marriage, gifts to the needy, the way we should pray (The Lord's Prayer), fasting, treasurer in Heaven, do not worry, judging others, patience in faith and keeping priorities straight. "As your first duty, keep on looking for His standard of doing right and for His will, and then all things necessary will be yours" (Matt. 5:33).

Finally, The Golden Rule – "Then you must practice dealing with others as you would like for them to deal with you" for this is the summing up of the law and the prophets.

Congregational Ethics
Working Together

Clergy burnout usually is ascribed to "The pastor is doing too much"; "He has too many irons in the fire"; "He won't delegate"; "He doesn't trust the congregation and must keep in control"; etc. One seldom hears one or another group from the congregation say, "What can we do to help him/her?"

Burnout and/or *clergy abuse* is not confined to one denomination. It is almost epidemic. For several decades now many denominations have developed and offered help to the minister and his family after the fact. Resource persons and conferences, materials and sometimes financial assistance are available to help the wounded recover.

Church congregations have responsibility, whether assumed or not, for prevention of a dysfunctional church family life that breeds a climate for clergy burnout and abuse. A headline news story read, "Clergy Burnout – The Cause: People Beating on Each Other." My family physician and colleague gave his version. "From where I sit listening to both ministers and church members, dissension occurs in a church when a person begins vying for power, and he becomes at odds with another person or group within the congregation. As members of competing groups turn to the minister as a mediator or counselor, he is soon caught in the middle. He becomes the problem and is expendable." Each of the competing groups wins until the next minister settles in with the real issues unsettled, soon to be repeated with new minister and his family as victims.

The beginning point for the congregation is to have a formal statement, such as a constitution and necessary by-laws to cover the essential relationships with each other, their employees and the community. Following the early church principle of organization, "as a need arose they organized to meet the need," provision will be made for necessary committees. No need – no committee. (Opinion: There will be no committee meetings in Heaven!) Policy statements, job descriptions, simple operational manuals may evolve and be helpful to outline *responsibility, authority, accountability,* and *liability.* The laws of the state and city may help determine the advisability of incorporation.

Many ideas of *what to do or not to do, the way we ought to do,* or *what Bigville is doing* will surface. An idea, cause or plan may be referred to the personnel, property, or fellowship committees, etc., for study and report of findings to the semi-governing body, such as deacons or elders for further study and report on recommendation.

Congregational ethics demand that the congregation have a plan of action for the calling or hiring of a minister. For some denominations this procedure is determined by a structure of assignment or appointment by another *ecclesiastical higher authority.*

If the congregation uses a *search committee,* by whatever name, that committee must not misinform the prospective staff member as to the spiritual health of the body, the mission of the church at the present time or make promises the congregation has not agreed upon. "Perish the thought," you say. Shame, shame, it happens too often. The minister's days are numbered as he walks into a hornet's nest of discord or misunderstanding. Study the questions in the last chapter on "Denominational Methods to Move Ministers" to think on the ethics of a search committee. The committee must be careful, too, in the report to the congregation to be sure adequate and accurate information concerning the prospective minister and other staff members is given well in advance of any vote that may be taken.

The Minister's Friend

Not all persons are gifted the same. Ministers and laypersons alike are responsible for the knowledge, power and resources that each possesses but are also responsible for what one ought to possess. Among many things these truths may mean we do not remain static in our spiritual development. The minister as well as the members must be discerning to these changing needs that affect our choice in relationships. Each staff member will naturally develop patterns of social life within his/her group. All need some close friends.

Read again "Essence of Fellowship," chapter 5.

At this point, the staff ministers, including the senior minister, should read again or better still study Chapter 7 under the leadership of the senior minister or someone chosen by him. This may result in the participants making suggestions for changes or additions to the policy makers of the congregation.

After six months as pastor, Tom went to the friend who had served as interim before he was called, and said, "Ed, the minister of education for five years has to go. He won't let me be the *pastor*. Members go to him in matters that should be brought to me." The friend responded, "No, Ed does not have to go, and both of you will be hurt if he does. So you ask him for a day alone to talk and pray through to an understanding." This they did and worked happily together for five years. Thirty years later the pastor again thanked the friend, saying, "Following your counsel that day has given me great joy, and to think I was about to blow it."

Harold was a dedicated but ill-informed deacon, church treasurer and Sunday School leader who usually opposed whatever the leadership suggested but was seldom successful. He was the minister's "thorn in the flesh." The pastor prayed fervently for him but more for himself that he would be understanding, gentle and patient. When Betty, age six, wanted to go to the circus, Harold hesitated to take her until the minister volunteered to go along. Many other gestures of friendship were made in the eight years. Upon the announcement of the minister's leaving, Harold embraced him and weeping on his shoulder said, "I love you like a brother." The pastor, weeping with him, responded, "Bless be the tie that binds our hearts." Through distance with few contacts that tender Christian love continued for fifty years until the death of the minister's friend.

In casual conversation members may behave unethically toward a minister. As they were leaving the church door after greeting the minister, the ten-year-old asked, "Are you and the preacher friends?" The father jovially answered, "Of course, son, what made you ask?" The boy said, "I like him, but some of the things I have heard you say at home about him made me wonder; that's all."

The member may not have intended to be hypercritical or to have his *idle words* so taken, but they were repeated to another in such vein and to another!

Here follows a litany (second definition: *a dreary listing*) of statements that could be true but are better left unsaid.

1. He eats too much and doesn't exercise.
2. You never can find him through the week.
3. He doesn't hear the question but always knows the answer.
4. He preaches the sermons of others.
5. He takes credit for any success but never blame for failure.
6. Confidential to him does not mean confidential.
7. He is always late and always in a hurry.

Contrast these negative comments with those of friendship and support:

1. He certainly seem to fit our needs now.
2. He really cares for us.
3. He is a part of a healing team.
4. Doctors respect him.
5. He is one of the best.
6. He wants to understand and respect our history.
7. He challenges us to be our best.

Mature ministers will appreciate expressions of love and gratitude they hear about former ministers. Knowing that the individual or congregation has the capacity to love, they are assured that they will soon be in that love-circle.

One scripture used at the beginning of this section referred to *burden bearing*. Paul suggests that burdens are lifted by those who are *spiritual* in contrast to those who are yet carnal, gratifying the cravings of their lower nature. (Read Galatians 5:16-6:2).

Among the burdens that the minister's friend may help lift:

1. Becoming acquainted with the membership and community leaders of other congregations.
2. The burden of family illness or personal health problems.
3. Helping children making adjustment to new friends.
4. Aging parents.
5. Chronic illness of family member.
6. Congregations sometimes have a higher expectation for children of the minister.
7. Children being rebellious or defiant from peer or parental pressure.
8. Parental discipline being too heavy.
9. Help protect minister or family from gossip.
10. Burden of minister's continued education.
11. Burden of children's education needs.
12. Knowledge of necessary local congregation history.
13. Burden of the mission and benevolent needs encountered weekly.
14. Time management for family, work, devotion, recreation, and rest.

How may one demonstrate that she/he is the minister's friend?

1. By affirming conversations with him or about him.
2. By rejoicing with the minister in signs of spiritual growth among members and/or a growing love in the fellowship.
3. By supporting in a personal or family crisis.
4. By trusting your minister in confiding your personal concerns.
5. By using her/his gifts, (talents or experience) to share the minister's vision and task to the glory of God.
6. By assuring the minister of appreciation for his/her ministry.
7. The friend does not demand excessive attention and time from the minister.
8. The friend is sensitive to the needs of the minister's family and, if possible, aid in alleviating some of the stress factors.
9. The friend will respect the privacy of the minister and family.
10. The friend will pray for the minister, remembering that prayer for another is the most *loving* thing you can do!

Ingratitude is the sin that causes the most sadness. Unexpressed gratitude is the sin that brings the most regret. Ministers sometimes are given so many favors they tend to react as though they are due them all. Ministers should express gratitude mannerly and in good taste. The friend will not give favors to manipulate for a position or power. And by no means will a respectable minister hint or ask for something the friend may have in a manner that is manipulative.

Wilford offered voluntarily to loan money for an indefinite time to clear a debt so the pastor could continue his education. When the minister was able to pay the note, it was returned, marked, "Paid in full as an investment in Christian education" – a minister's friend!

D. C. Simmons, merchant and banker, was a small boy when told by his old pastor, "Young man, if you ever make any money, remember that the best investment you can make of it is in the lives of young ministers and missionaries." In an interview for the biography of Dr. Dana, Simmons said, "I've remembered that! I have made a lot of investments in my time. I have paid for the education of more than one hundred ministers and missionaries. I can count on the fingers of one hand those that have gone wrong, and I can testify that the word of my old friend is true. Those were the best investments I have ever made."

Mr. Simmons became the minister's friend to his pastor, H. E. Dana, at Utica, Mississippi, when he offered to pay for Dana's education through seminary. He continued until the former pastor had earned the Th.M., Th.D. and two post graduate degrees. Dana considered the money as a loan, and when he began to "pay back," Mr. Simmons would not have it – so Dana established a "D. C. Simmons New Testament Library Fund," depositing money in it until he considered his financial debt paid. Dr. Dana taught seminary students more than thirty years, wrote seventeen books, and co-authored the *Dana-Mantey Greek Grammar* used by scholars all over the world. More than 10,000 ministers and missionaries have been blessed by Dana's friend. Dr. Dana was my seminary president, professor, advisor, encourager and intimate friend. I felt our relationship was as father and son. After his death, his daughter confirmed this by saying, "I am sure you realize that my father considered you the son he never had. I am so glad you learned to know and love each other."

Chalk up another one for D.C. Simmons. And how about his old pastor who planted the seed of generous friendship for ministers and missionaries? But when we get the thousands of the Dana bunch together, the Lord will be leading the class.

Dr. Dana carried this poem in his billfold.

> You may plant your life by the river's brink
>   Where the limpid waters flow:
> You may plant your life in the shaded glen
>   Where no chilling tempests blow:

You may plant your life on the mountain's height
　　'Neath the smile of the arching blue
You may plant your life where you will, my friend,
　　Since that choice is left to you:
But if I am to choose the course of my life,
　　As the field of the world I behold,
I will plant my life in the heart of the young
　　To bear ten-thousand fold.

The emphasis of this epilogue is not by chance or by my choice. In my delightful journey by the grace of God for these seventy years since ordination, hundreds of pastors in their public introductions have said, "He is the minister's friend," or "He is my pastor." To be called either is an honor and a humbling experience. I do know that wherever I have been in the geography of God's will, I have tried to serve with a shepherd-servant heart, and I rejoice when it has been evident!

Yes, your minister needs a friend, and it may well be that the Lord has placed you where you can be just that, *The Minister's Friend*.

So, if there is any persuasive power in love,
if we have any common share of the spirit,
if you have any tenderness and sympathy,
fill up my cup of joy by living in harmony,
by fostering the same disposition in love,
your hearts beating in unison,
your minds set on one purpose
Keep fostering the same disposition
that Christ Jesus had.
Philippians 2:1ff

"The Lord bless you, and keep you:
The Lord make his face to shine upon you,
and be gracious unto you:
The Lord lift up his countenance upon you,
and give you peace."
Numbers 6:24-26

Resource Suggestions

Preacher Behave now in the sixth printing has always been considered by the author as a practical handbook for young ministers. By no means it is not the only word or the last word but a good word and a right word for many ethical relationships. You may desire to know what others think, as most truth seekers do, here are some starters.

Consult your state or national denominational specialists.

Visit bookstores that carry more than one denominational line of products. These are but illustrations of what you will find. In examining books check Contents, Introduction or Preface, appendices, and bibliography. There has been a proliferation of new books on ethics. Take care!

• Joe E. Trull & James E. Carter. *Ministerial Ethics, Being a Good Minister in a Not-So Good World.* Broadman and Holman Publishers. One of the most complete, practical, scholarly and timely books yet written on the subject.

• *Broken Trust: Confronting Clergy Sexual Misconduct.* Christian Life Commission, Baptist General Convention of Texas, 333 N. Washington, Dallas, TX 75246-1798, www.bgct.org. Most comprehensive-including the nature and prevalence of clergy sexual abuse, Wounded Victims, the prevention of and response to *Clergy Sexual Abuse and a Covenant of Clergy Sexual Ethics*, written by Joe Trull, Editor of *Christian Ethics Today, A Journal of Christian Ethics*, printed in part on next page.

A Covenant of Clergy Sexual Ethics
Used by permission, Christian Life Commission, Dallas, Texas

The purpose of a covenant of sexual ethics for ministers are threefold: (1) to provide a framework for upholding sexual integrity among ministers; (2) to support and protect ministers by defining ethical norms; and (3) to establish a process for achieving justice, reconciliation, and healing.

Definition of Sexual Misconduct by Ministers

• Sexual relations outside of marriage;
• Unwanted or inappropriate physical contact;
• All other sexually oriented or suggestive behaviors, such as overt and covert seductive speech and gestures;
• The use of pornography.

Covenant

As a minister called to serve God and God's people, I commit myself to the following norms of ethical conduct, for which I am accountable to God, to my colleagues in ministry, and to the church in which I serve.

• I will demonstrate sexual integrity in ministry by understanding, respecting, and observing the boundaries of sexual misconduct as defined above.

• I will nurture my physical, emotional, and spiritual health, maintain enriching friendships and build strong relationships with my spouse and family.

• I will develop relationships with God, my spouse, and close friends who encourage accountability and protect against temptation.

• I will recognize the special power afforded me in the pastoral office by never abusing that power in ways that violate the personhood of another human being, by assuming responsibility for maintaining proper boundaries in church staff/church member relationships, and by acknowledging that the congregant is always in a vulnerable position.

• I will avoid all forms of sexual exploitation and/or harassment in my professional and social relationships, even if others invite such behavior or involvement.

• I will not seek or accept sexual favors.

• I will exercise good judgment in professional and private conduct by avoiding situations, which create the appearance of sexual misconduct.

• I will assume responsibility to report any reliable evidence of sexual misconduct by another minister to the appropriate person or committee.

- I will submit to the policies and procedures of the church when an allegation of sexual misconduct has been made, recognizing the importance of justice and due process procedures.
- As I seek to fulfill my responsibilities as a minister, I will strive to embody servant-leadership in all my relationships and to pattern my life and ministry after the example of Jesus Christ.

A Word of Assurance
"My God in His tender Mercy will meet me at every corner."
Psalm 59:10 Paraphrased

HE IS THERE!
Just the moment you were born
There stood the Father looking on
And He was pleased with what
He knew that you could be.
Very good, the Father said,
I will steer your course ahead
At every turn in the road
Count on me.

As an acorn becomes a tree
Just as surely you will be
Endowed with power to grow
To something great.*
You are important to His plan
So do the very best you can
At every turn in the road
Celebrate!

When there's trouble and there's pain
It will never be in vain
For we cannot get beyond His loving care
God will strengthen and will bless
In the struggle and the stress
At every turn in the road
He'll be there!

But in the bright and sunny days
When life is moving smooth and good
We count our blessings one by one
And offer praises as we should
Though we cannot always understand
He ever helps by His Strong Hand
At every turn in the road
He is there!

He is there! He is there!
At every turn in the road He is there.
In His mercy and His love
He will meet you from above
At every turn in the road,
He is there!

J.C.H. circa 1985
* "Service to others constitutes greatness" –Jesus. (Mark 9:35)